Ruu Ruu & 100% Parade
Story©2018 Ruu*Ruu

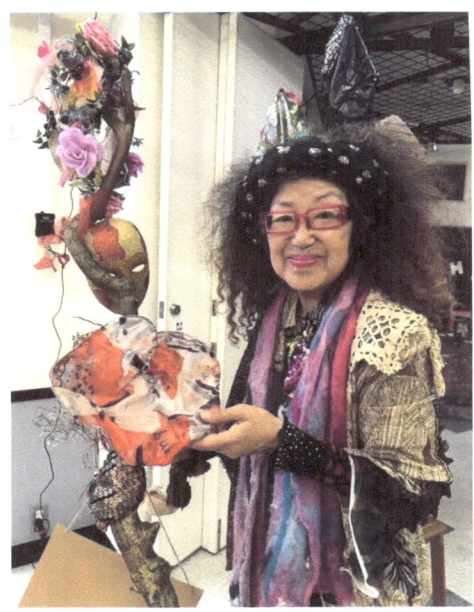

Written by Della Burford
from notes taken when in Mexico
Compilation & Design Della Burford

with Ruu*Ruu's consultation

Thanks for all the friends
who provided photos & energy.
Thanks to all those who helped with
the 100% Project in so many ways.
Thanks to Dale Bertrand at

Azatlan Publishing
ISBN 978-1-927825-09-9

Introduction

For 30 years Ruu*Ruu had designed hat and costumes. She designed a lot of clothes for musicians such as the Rock Star Kiyoshiro Omawano. She loved shiny fabrics and different designs. In 1993 her son was born and this started a transition to a more natural way of life. In 1999 she had a hat Exhibition called "flower bloom.-.dream bloom -. heart bloom- chapeau de brilliant at Wakayama Shinwakaura Bland Bintang. Her hats even then were in the dream and beautiful flower realm. She then had an Exhibition "When the bliss, to the here and now" at Osaka Minami Gallery COMO. In 2000 she had an Exhibition "Dream of the Primordial" which had dream in the title again.

In 2007 she had an exhibition "Song of Celebration Festival of Song" at the Shibuya Tokyo Kono House. In 2000 she had a 2 person exhibition with a flower arrangement artist. Sogetsu Morikawa Edaen. In 2008 was show"Germination" . As you can see most of the titles have to do with Flowers, Dreams Growth and Bliss.

All of these themes seem to culminate in a dream in 2008 when she was making ethereal hats for the Angels. She was a hatmaker in heaven. This inspired her to make hats for people to show their angelic, and higher selves. To be their own champion.

As serendipity has it after the Big earthquake in 2011 she met Kazuko Asaba and heard her tell "The Magical Earth Secrets" story by myself (Della Burford). She really related to the theme "to love and protect the earth" and all the little people of the Rainbow who were in the story to tell the Secrets to the little Eagle Child to get its colors and power back. They decided to collaborate and she started to make the costumes and got many artists, and creators to join in the play of the story. They performed with the group 100% Parade. This book mostly chronicles that journey.

100% Parade artist and creators dress up in fantastic costumes and Parade the streets with a particular theme in mind such as Peace, Love, Happiness, Creativity. Ruu* Ruu is part of this group.

The Costume of Ruu*Ruu are are very alive & vibrant in the preformance of the story of "Magical Earth Secrets", that they call"Majical Rainbow" They have performed it for the Earth Day Celebration in Tokyo and also at the Kanazawabunko Festival in Yokohama.

In 2015 they had a Parade and Performance celebrating and Ruu Ruu visualized people parading as flowers and painting the streets. In 2016 they had a "Kunitachi" Parade honoring the Rock Star Ruu*Ruu used to design for Kiyoshiro Imawano. There were models in costumes like him. Ruu*Ruu designed many costumes with colorful fabrics and flowers to bring out the champion and higher self in many Paraders. Brazilian dancers, Flamengo dancers, and children singing and playing instruments came. The culminated with a performance of "Magical Earth Secrets" – Majical Rainbow'. This same year they had a performance at the Yoyogi Square.

In 2017 it was the first year they could not Parade because of the weather. But like true artist they improvised and created a Magic fantasy environment inside. Many artists, creators, and people with food and crafts joined in the time of magic. It was a time of Cooperation.

In spring of 2018 with Ruu*Ruu's lightning clothing they performed at the end "Majical Earth.". In 2018 (we) Della Burford and Dale Bertrand went to Japan to see the live show at the KanzawabunkoI Festival. We want to thank Ruu*Ruu and Kazuko Asaba for choosing to highlight "Magical Earth Secrets" and all the creators and artists This has meant a lot to us to have you share this with this part of the world. We loved what you are all doing there and thus have put this book together as a thank you gift to all of you. Keep on Parading for a better world! This may not be perfect or complete but we have done our best from the other side of the world.
     Love, Della Burford

Index Page

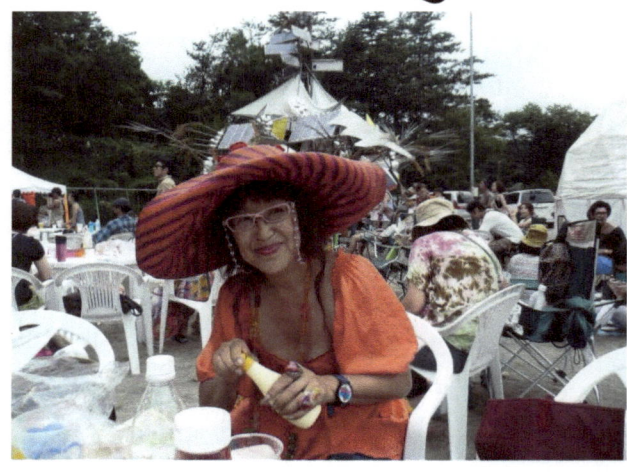

Ruu*Ruu & 100% Parade

	Introduction	p2/3
	Dream Hats Ruu*Ruu's Hats	p6
2007	"Song of Celebration" – First Parade	
2009	Parade & Live show at Yoyogi Park Tokyo	
2010	– Paris.– Matsuri	p11
2012	100% Parade "Love & Peace"	p9
2013	100% Parade Tokyo	p15
	"Love and Protect the Earth" Performance "Majical Rainbow" Adapted from "Magical Earth Secrets – Della Burford	
	Kanazawabunko Live Show	p16
2015	100% Parade Kunitachi Parade	p21
2015	Ruu*Ruu, Kazuko, Della and Dale meet in Mexico	p26
2016	100% Parade – Kunitachi Parade "Creativity" In memory to Kiyoshiro Imawanu Performances "Majical Rainbow	p27
2017	100% Parade "Cooperation" Parade inside because of typhoon Performance "Majical Rainbow"	p42
2018	Lightning Show of Fashion Performances "Majical Rainbow	p51
2018	Majical Rainbow at Kanzawabunko Festival	p53
2019	Working on "Miracle Galaxy costumes	

Della Burford, Ruu Ruu & Kazuko Asama meet in Puerto Vallarta 2015

We are starting here as this is when we first
*met Ruu*Ruu and Kazuko Asaba and*
I knew there should be a book on each one.

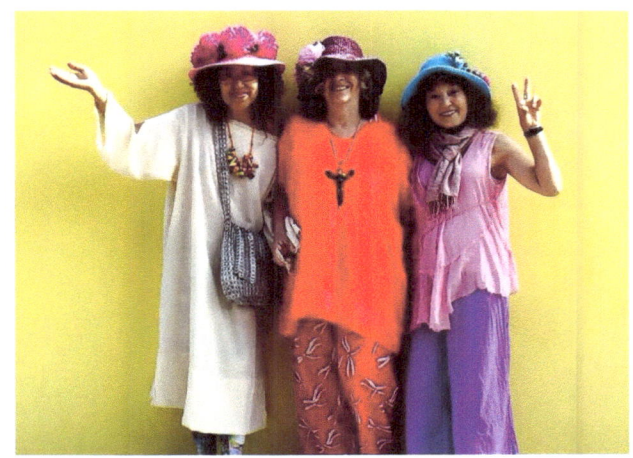

Ruu Ruu, Kazuko Asaba & Della*

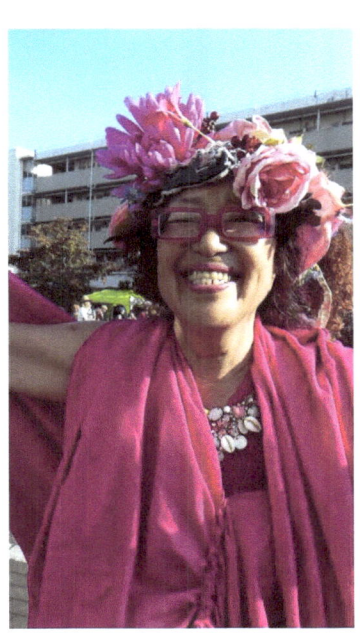

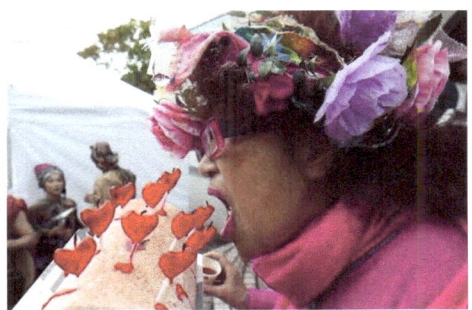

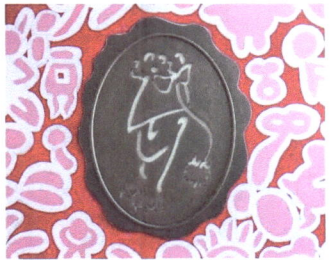

Ruu*Ruu's Dream Hats

Ruu*Ruu started of making hats about 30 years ago.. One day she had a dream. She saw a Well Rui Hats which were a golden in a dream. Inspired and impressed by this dream hats became the vocation of Ruu because of the impressive dream. The Hat boutique of Ruu was originally in heaven. The audience of Ruu*Ruu was not a human world, but celestial angels. The hat is a crown which represent people who live a life like an angel, like a goddess, like a champion .. a "god ornament". She makes individual hats for people to be champions in life. —
as explained by Ruu Ruu.

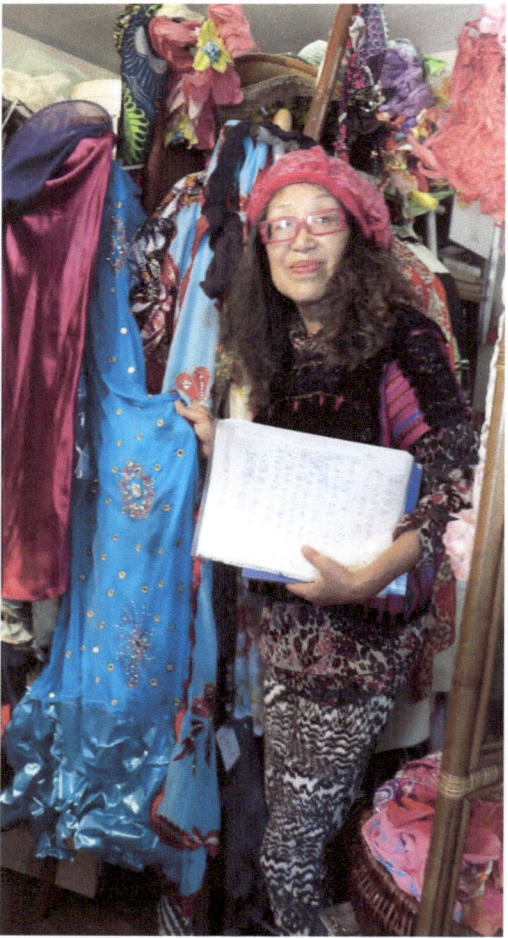
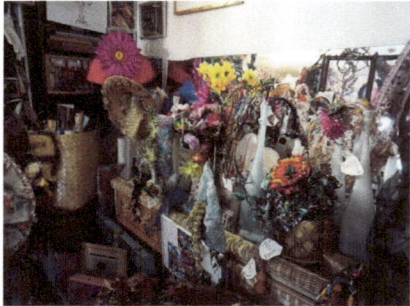
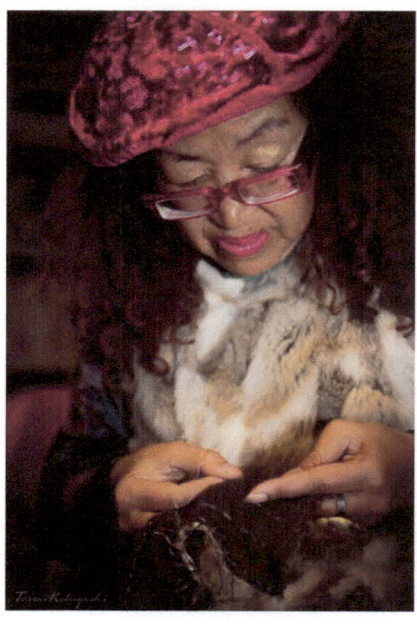

Designing Dream Hats

Ruu Ruu was told in a dream to make "God Ornaments". She began to make ethereal costumes and hats to help people to go to their highest selves.

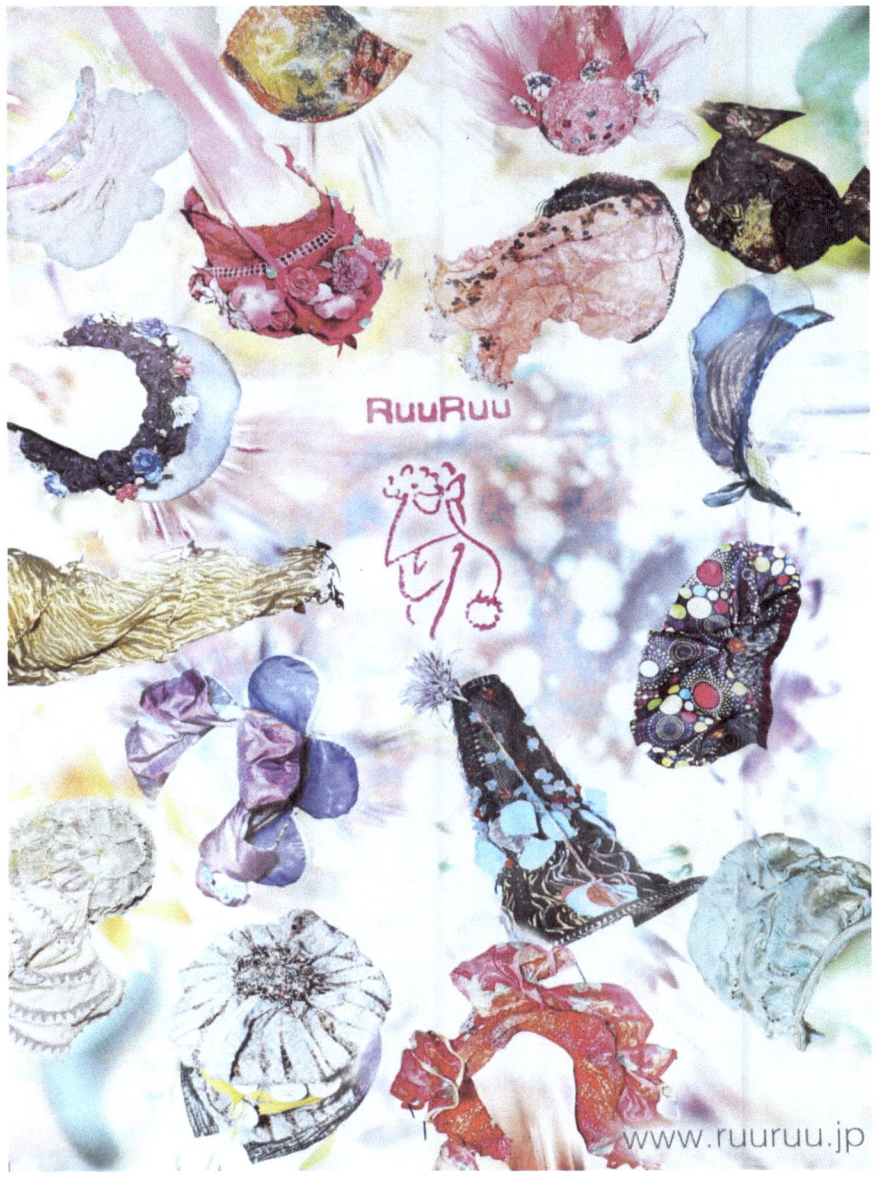

100% Parade 2007
Parade of Peace & Love!

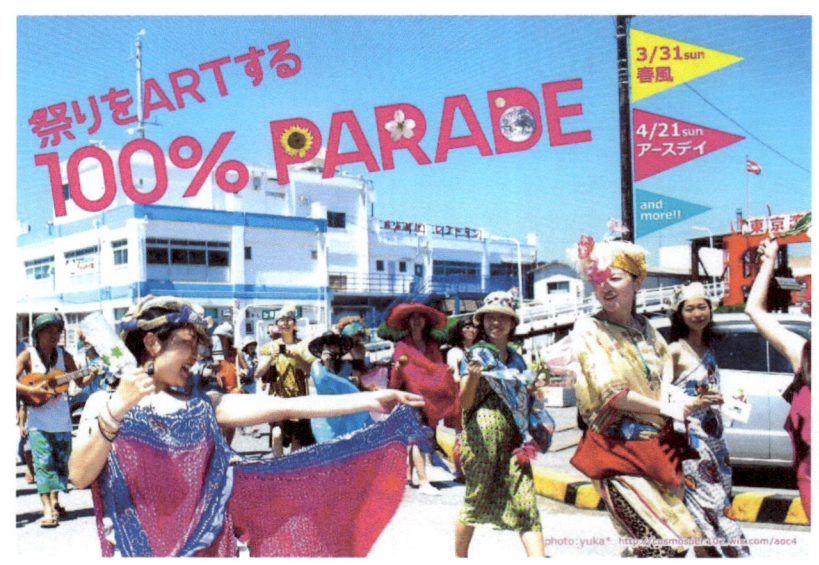

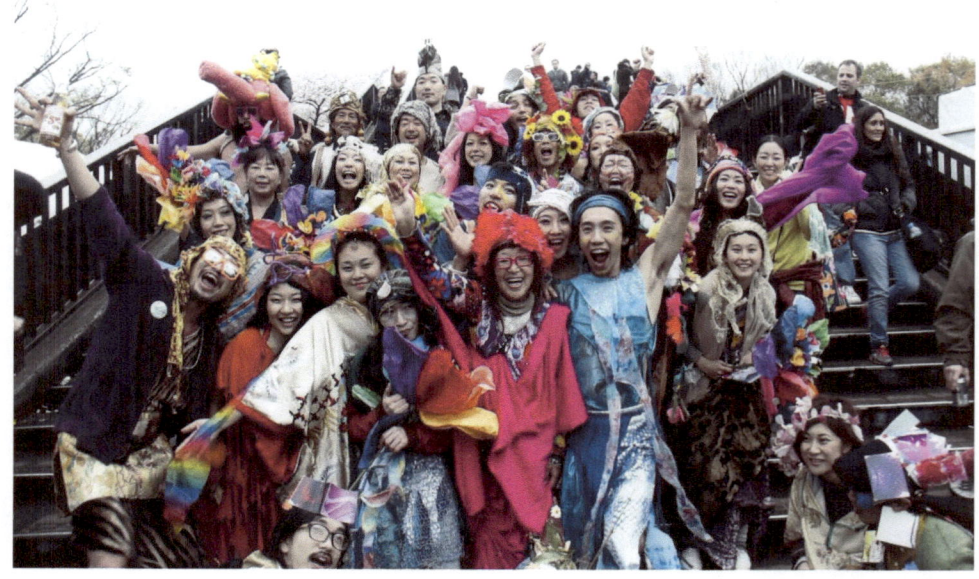

2008 100% Love and Peace Parade

100% LOVE and PEACE PARADE

かぶりもの
Chaco
KAKO/anuenue
Ruu Ruu

マイム
かず

サーカス
あずさ

ダンス
火の鳥
Ikuyo
Meena
ゆい
あさのゆうこ

装飾
Hibiki

音楽
Kaya
熊谷もん
Kengoman
せいちゃん
達川葉子
マーレーズ
ひねもす

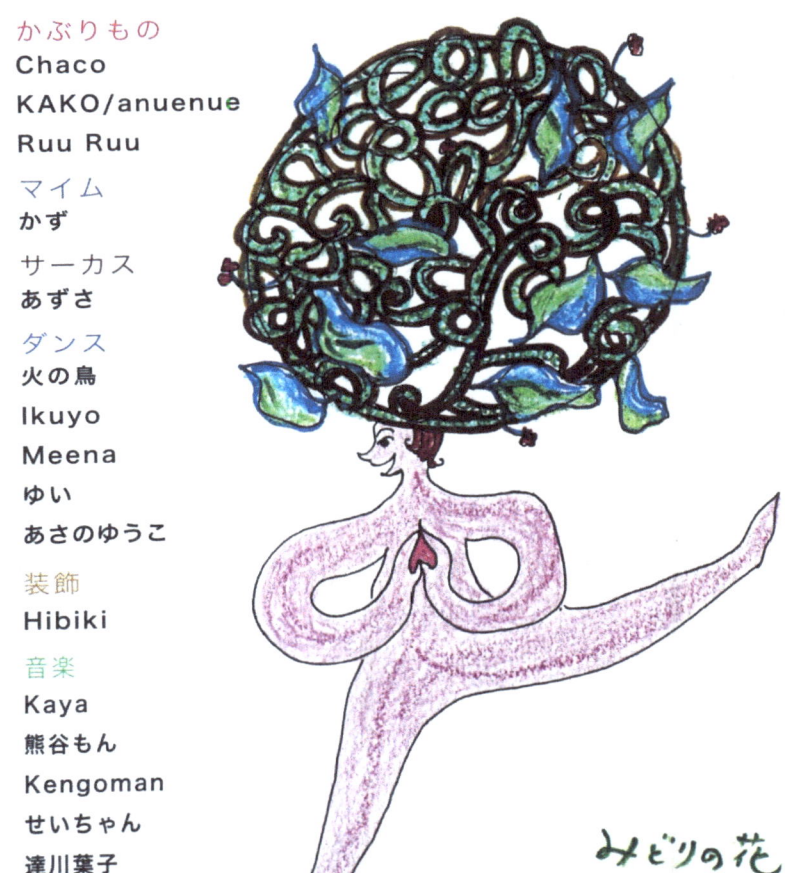

みどりの花
Ruu

100% Parade photos

The dancing and music is enjoyed by all!

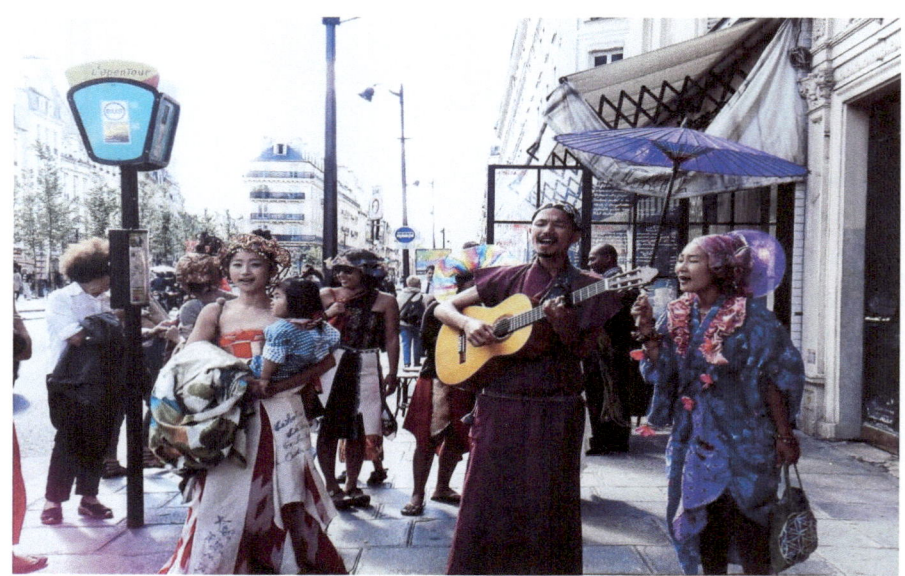

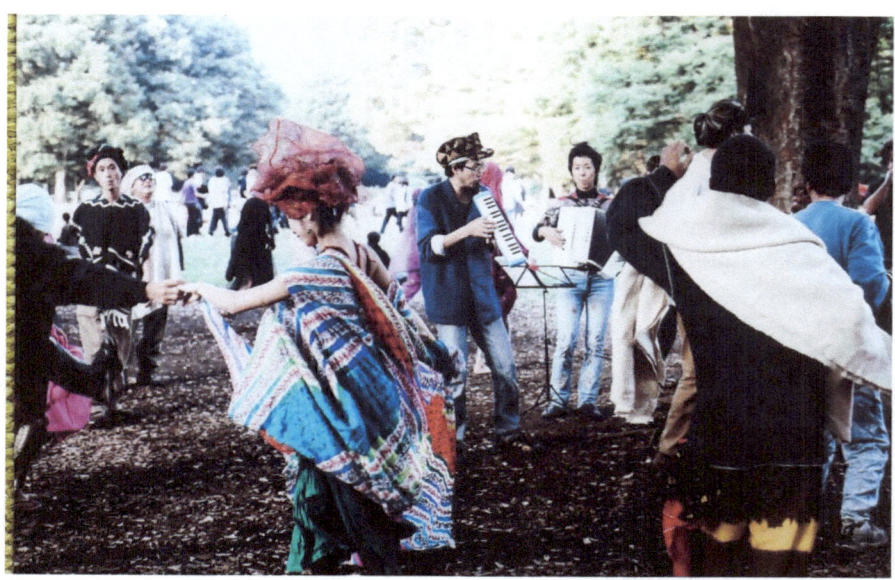

Matsuri in Paris
Espace Culturel Bertin Poiree and Les Voutes

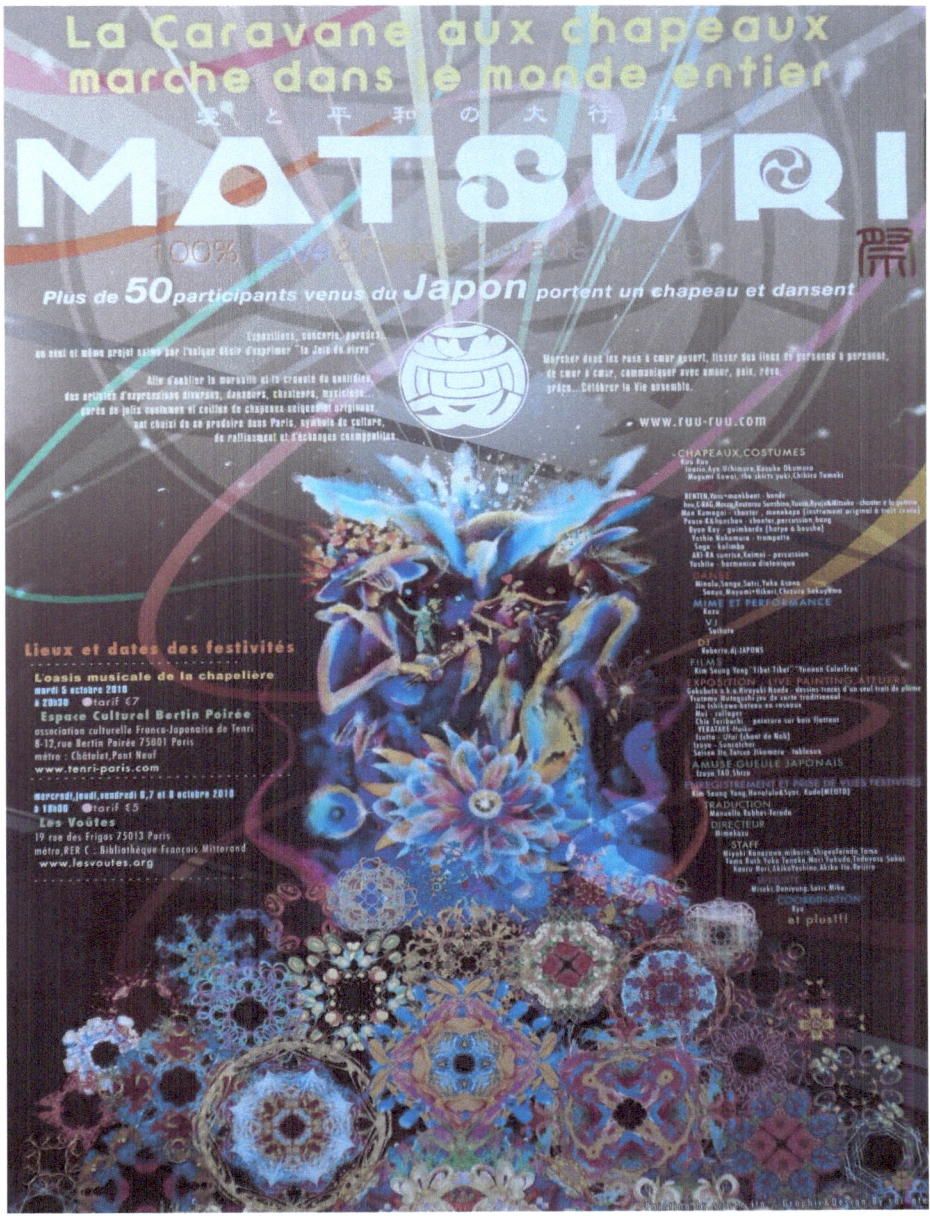

Matsuri

La Caravane aux chapeaux marche
dans le monde entier - 100% Parade

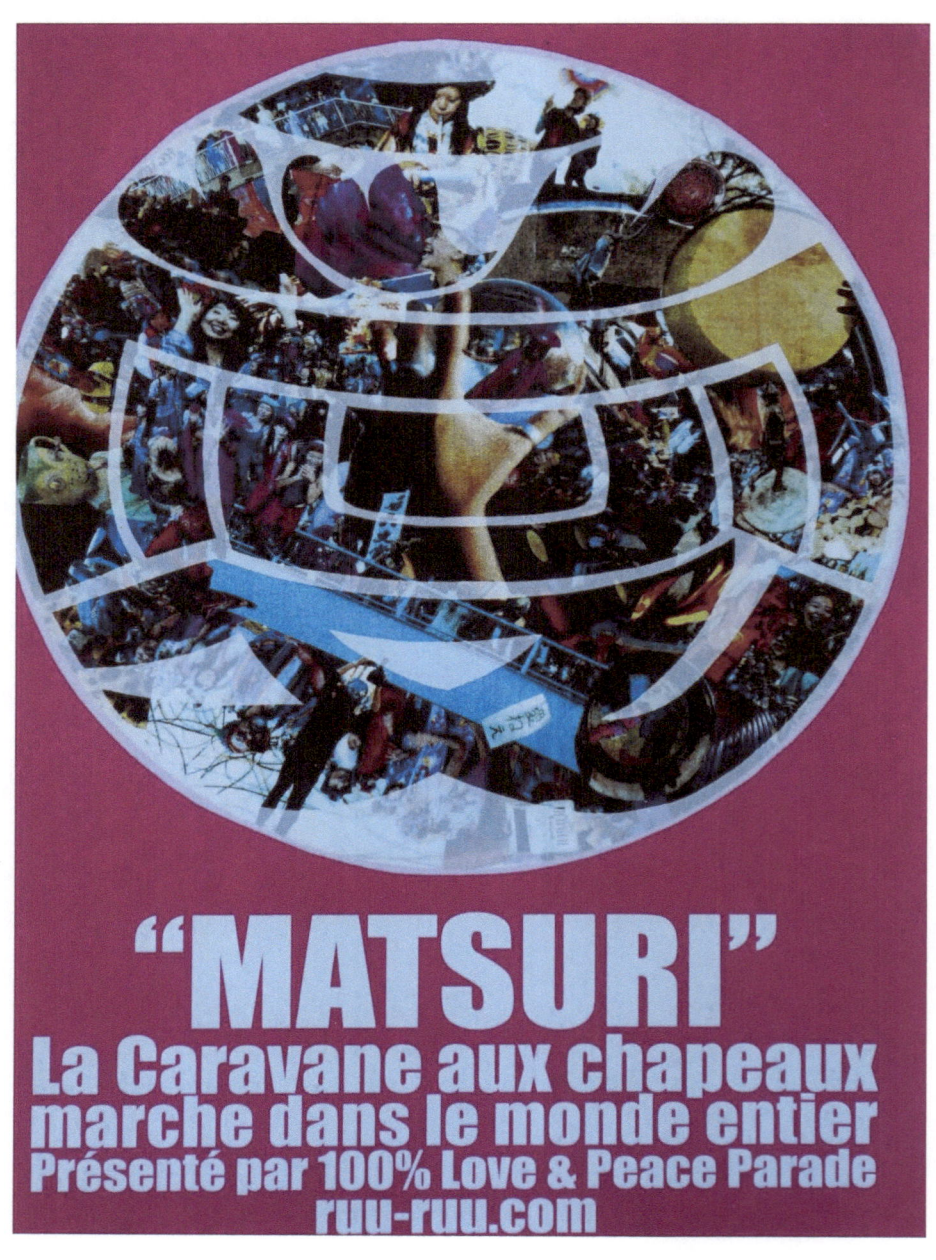

Some of the first Paraders 2012

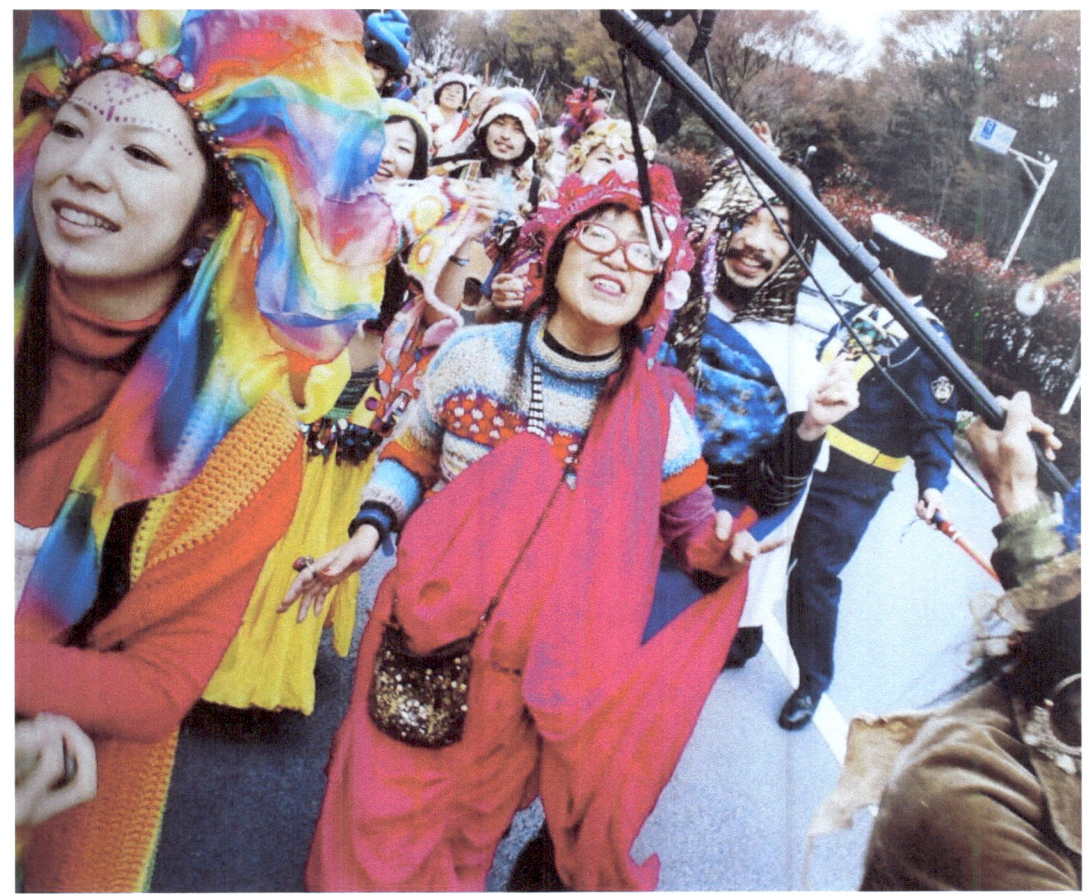

Magical Earth Secrets - Della Burford

Love and protect the Earth .. the story of Magical Earth tells of the Eagle Child who has lost its power and color because of pollution and how it gets its power back by connecting to the Elements of the Earth, Water, Sun, Air and Stars. A message for ALL!

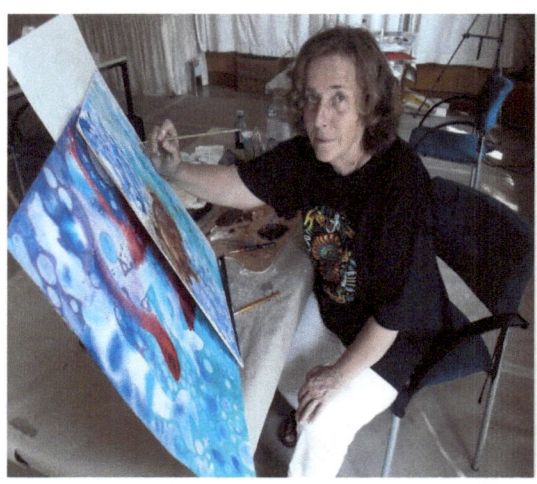

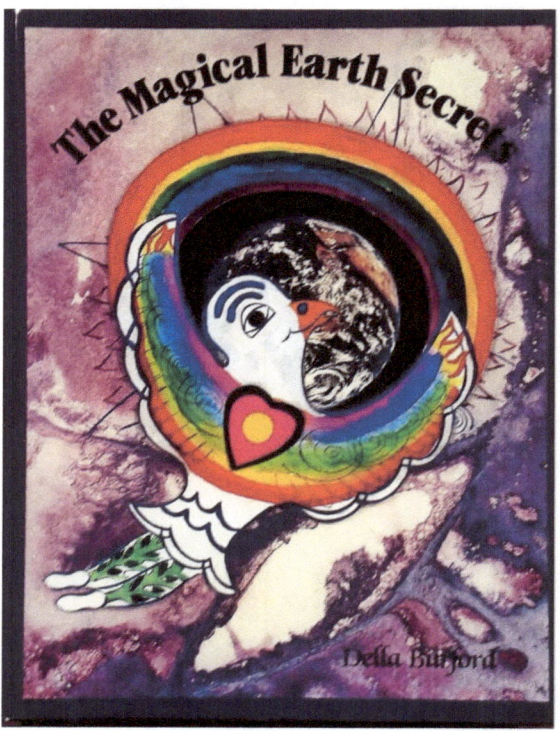

2013 Performance - Japan- Yotsuya Art Complex Centre -Majical Rainbow
(from Magical Earth Secrets by Della Burford)

photo by Masanao Showjit Sugyama

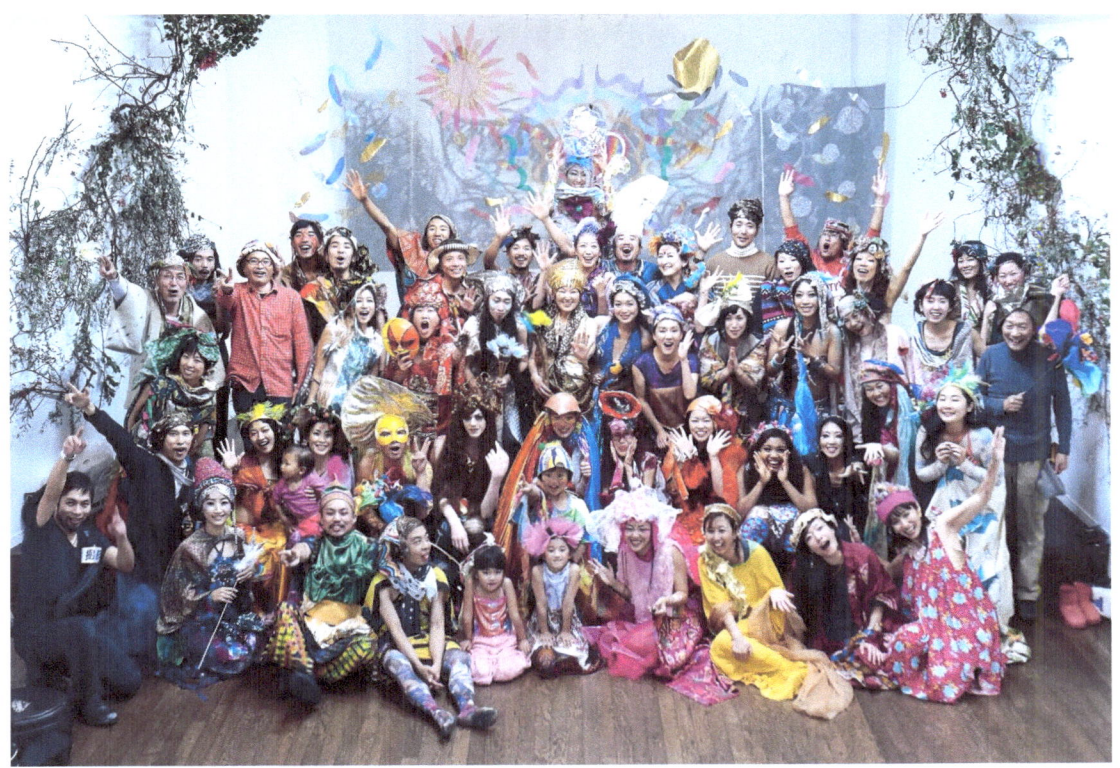

Majical Rainbow at the Kanazawabunko Festival 2013

Story/Painting by Author Della Canada Burford from Magical Earth Secrets published by the Western Canada Wilderness Commitee Production & Costumes- Ruu*Ruu

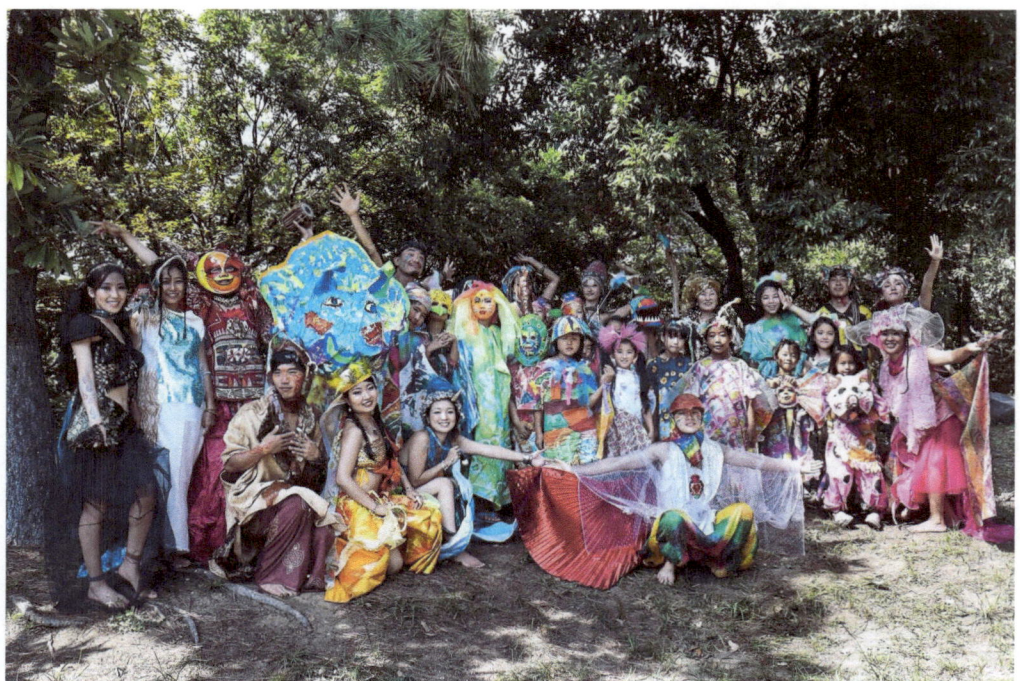

Collages inspired by Della Burford's book "Magical Earth Secrets" - made by Ruu*Ruu

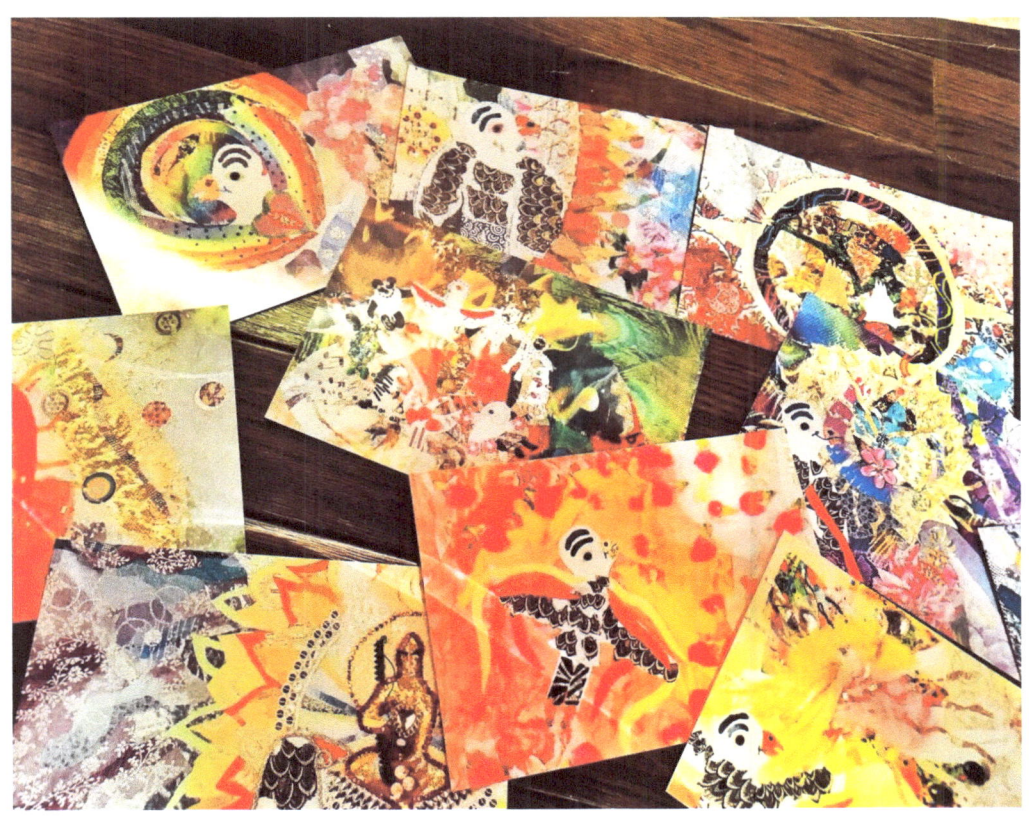

Parade 2014

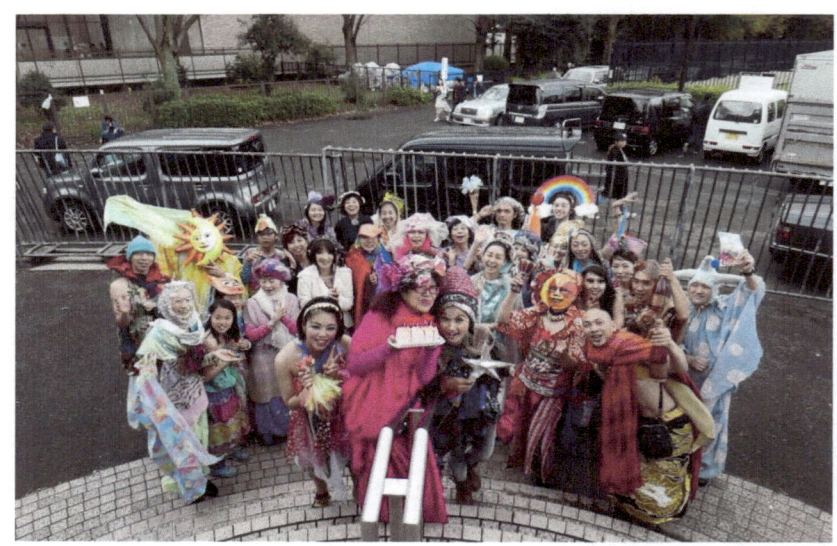

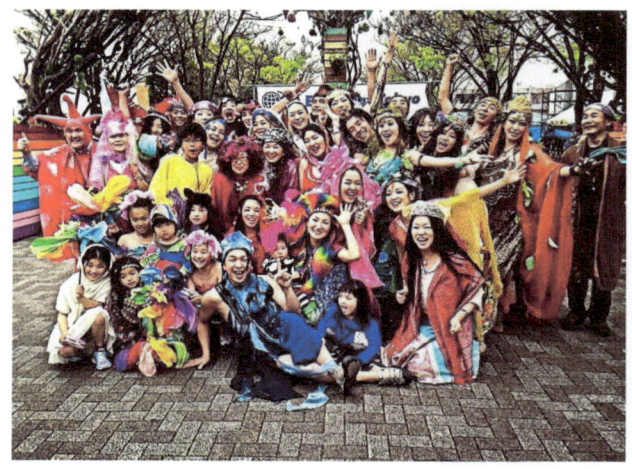

2014 Bringing Rainbow Wings from Magical Earth Secrets - Majical Rainbow to downtown Tokyo

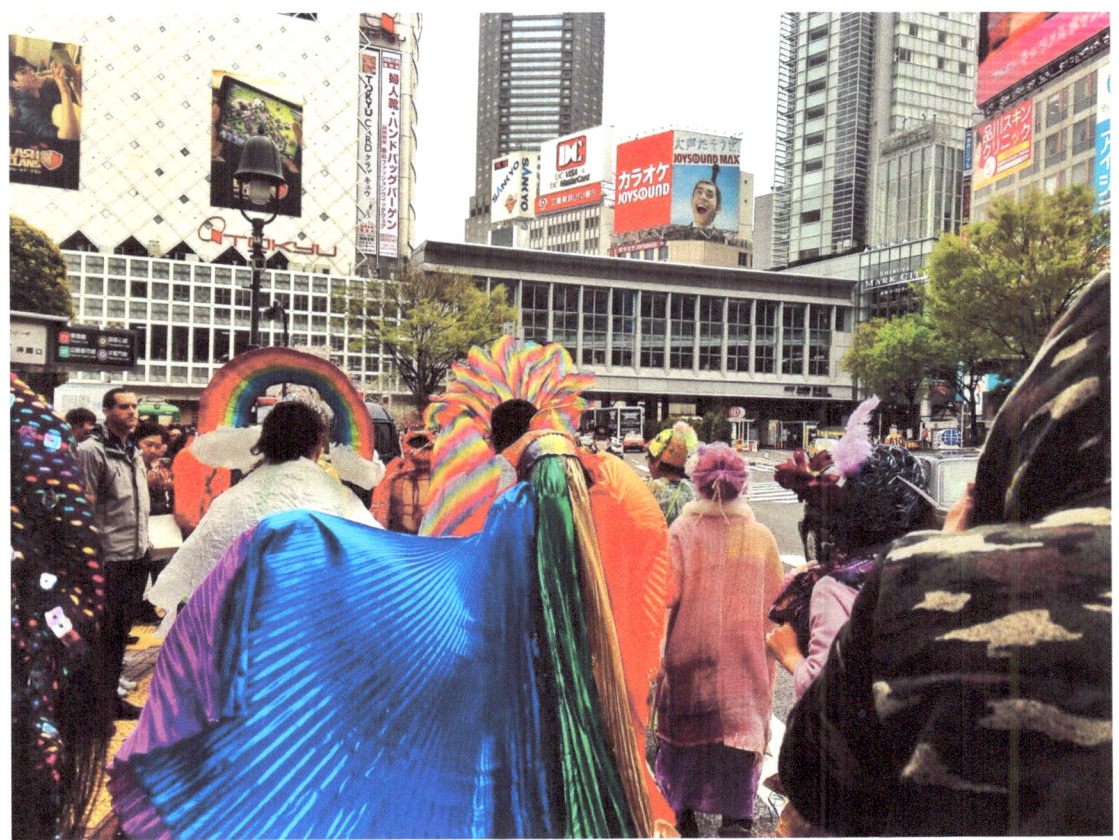

In Love at the Parade

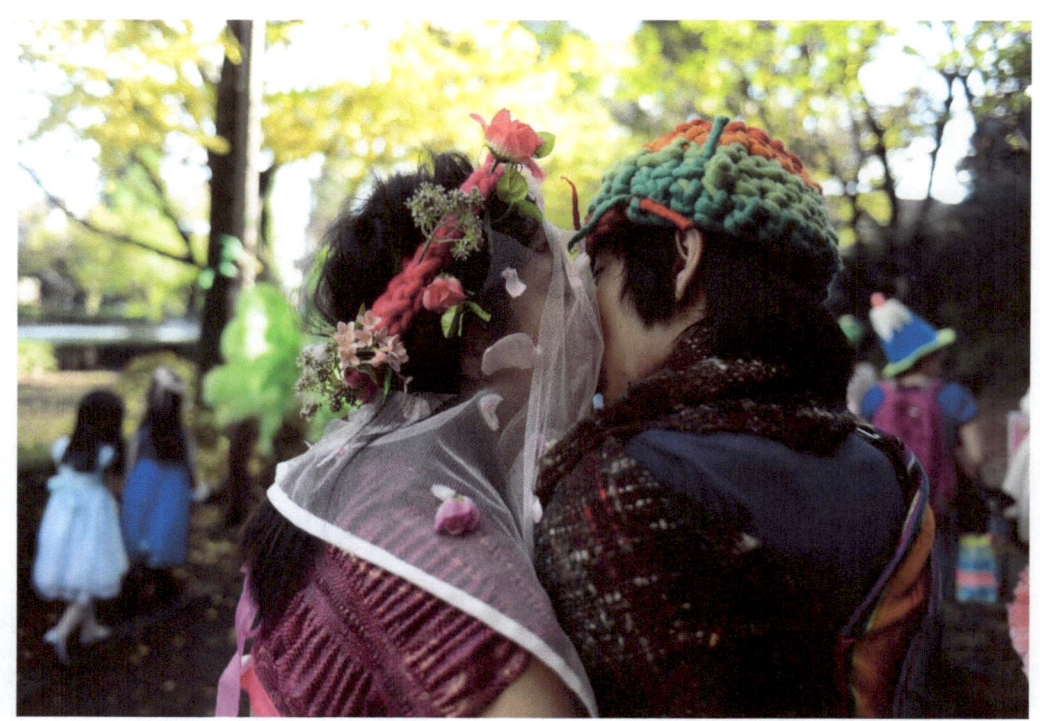

"As well as needing good earth, clean water and the sun, you and all people need love to grow" .. quote from Lovewind speaking in the book "Magical Earth Secrets"

2015 Ruu*Ruu*

What is the Parade?
A painting that comes alive!

Ruu ruu says: "You can experience the phenomenon, not the dream, live the happiness that might be a dream! Live freedom! Joy can be shared. People can also bloom thing! I want to bloom full of people of flowers. I want to bloom the smile of flowers. It is colorful and I want to paint a powerful painting in the street. Cherry blossoms in bloom is like someone dyed and the world rose in the spring, I want to bloom the people of the flowers in the parade in the fall."

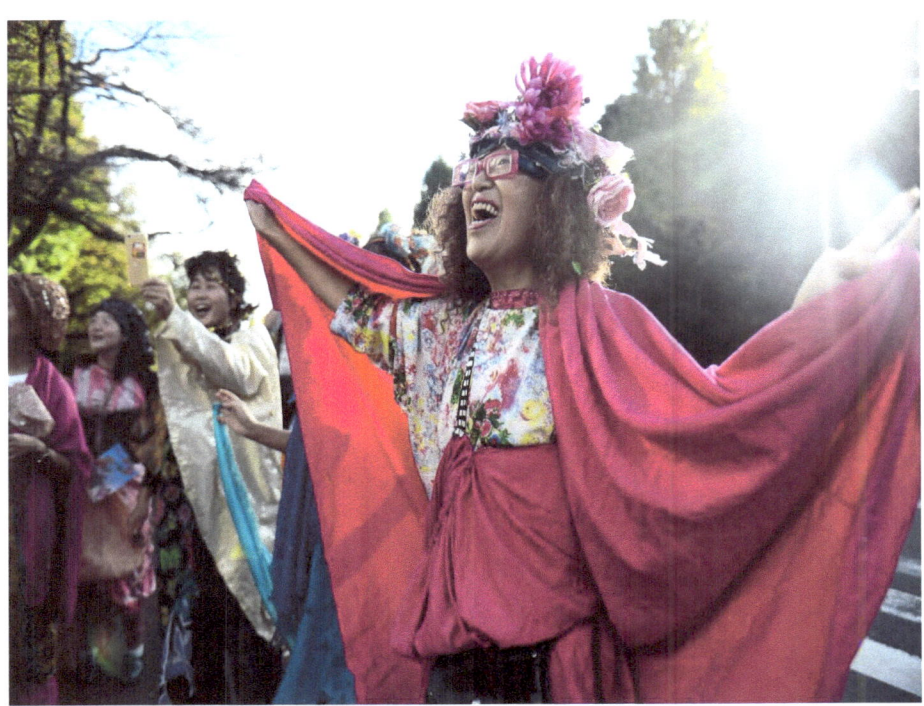

2015 Kunitachi Parade

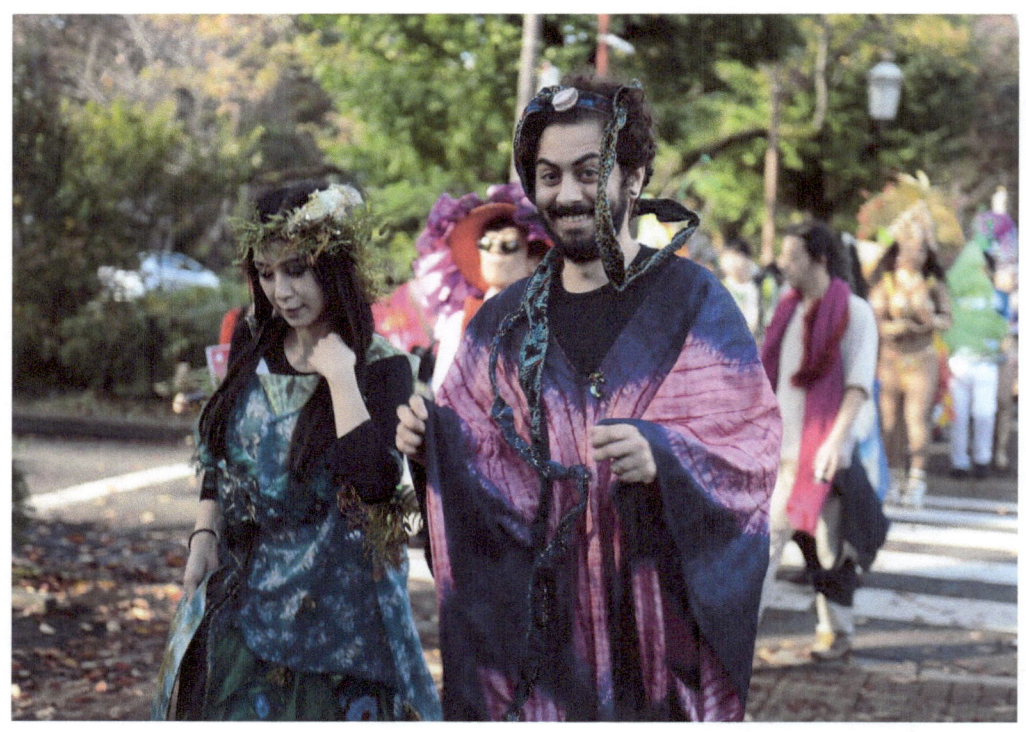

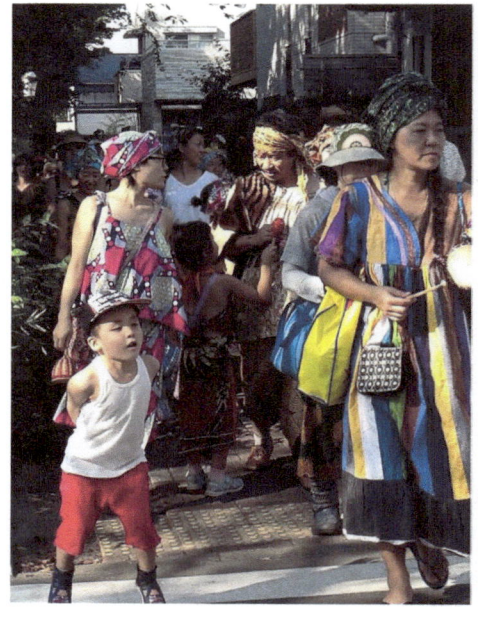

2015 Kunitachi Parade

This Parade starts at main, goes down university street straight leading to the south from the National Railway Station. It is a sight of colorful people walking and filling the street, it is like a paintings that has become alive! Art and fashion, culture and creativity are part of the festival, it is the "Kunitachi Parade! Photo Hanta Arits.

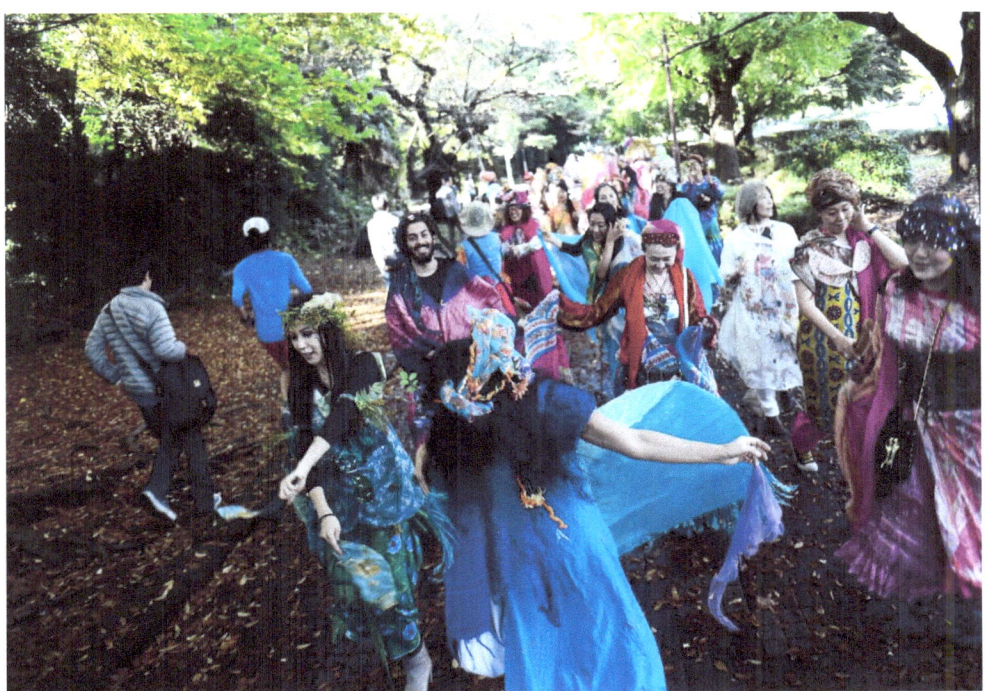

2015 Parade walking only in Joy and with Hope

RuuRuu says, " 100% PARADE started 10 years ago.
Parade just begun, so that you Yuki followed forever.
And from here, in every land of the earth, what will happen
is fun "Sampo". We are happy we live in a country where
people can walk in only joy, and we are filled with hope.

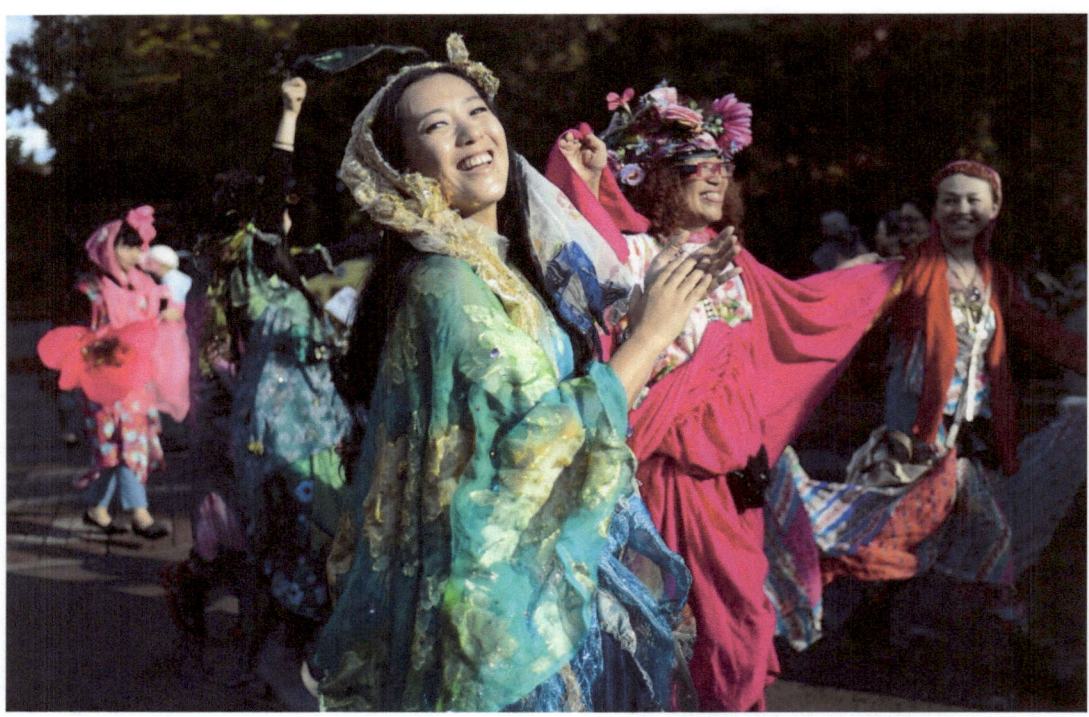

2015 - Storytelling in Mexico at a Children's English School - Ruu*Ruu, Kazuko & Della

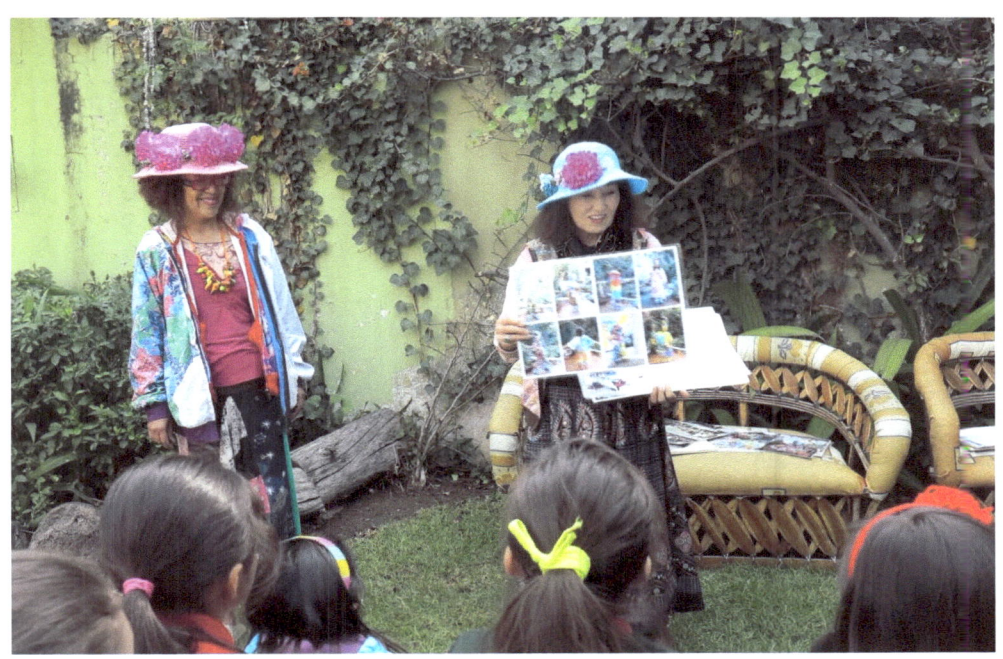

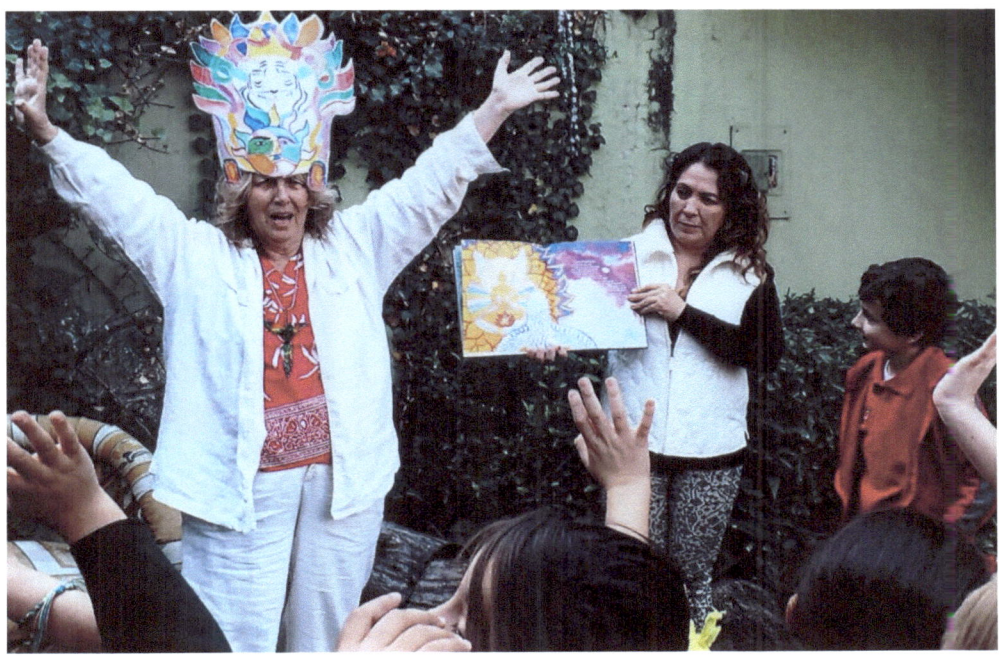

2013 Majical Rainbow (adaptation of Magical Earth Secrets - Yoyagi Square

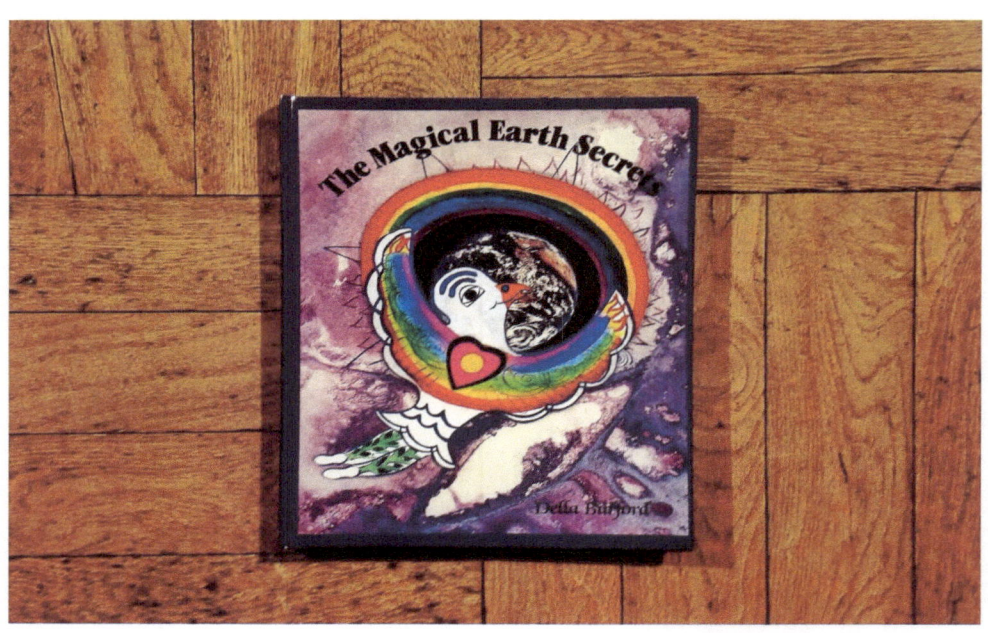

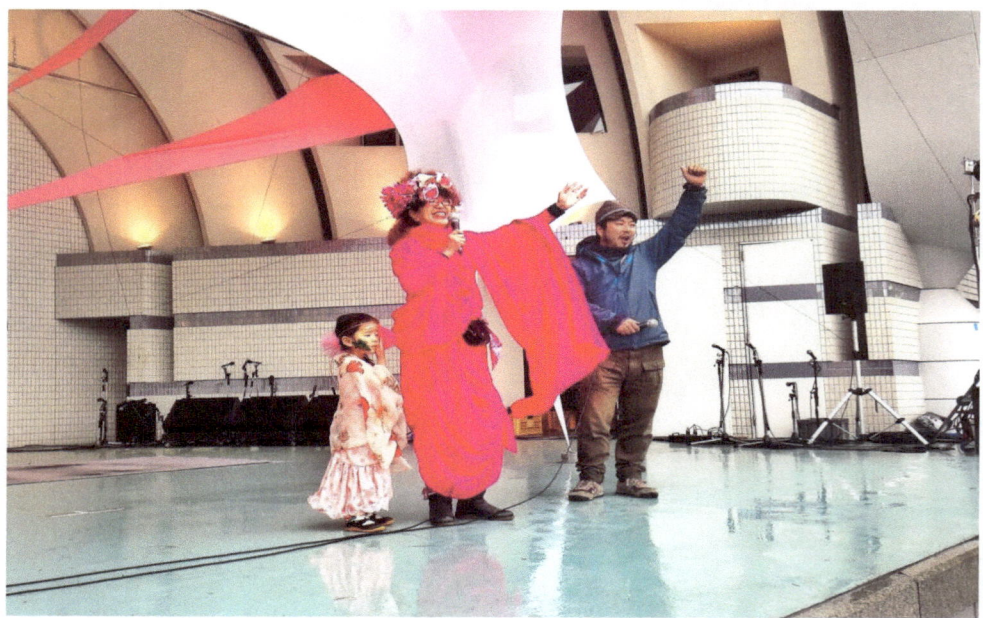

Ruu*Ruu at Yoyogi Park Event Square

Kiyoshiro Imawano costumes on Parade - in memory

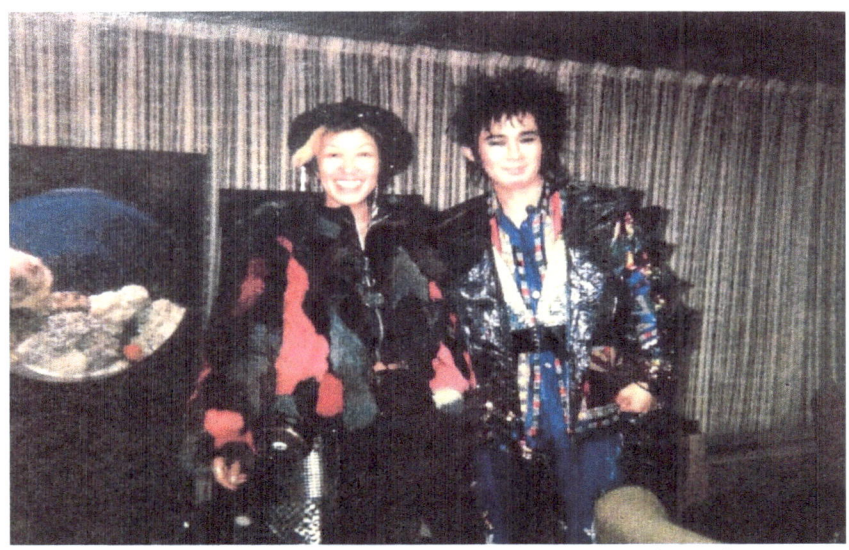

Ruu Ruu and Kiyoshiro Imawano who she designed cotumes for his concerts.

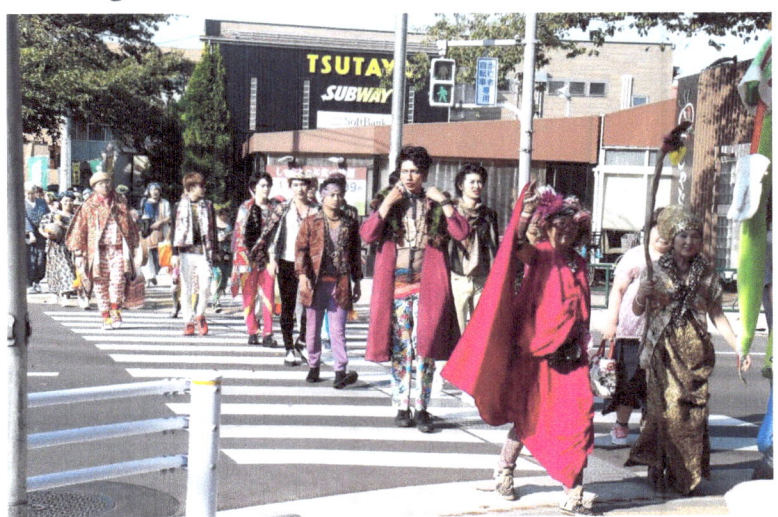

Ruu*Ruu made costumes for models like the ones for the Rock Star

We will transform to Kiyashiro Owanu for the parade! Thanks to the costume by Ruu*Ruu

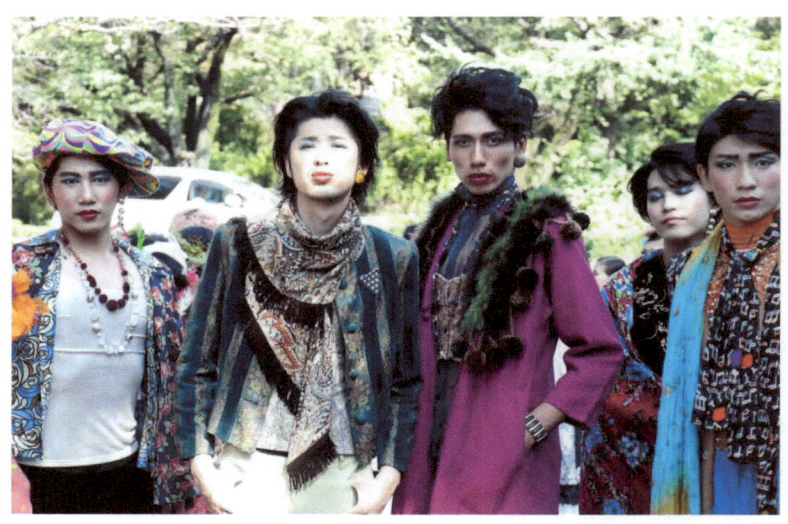

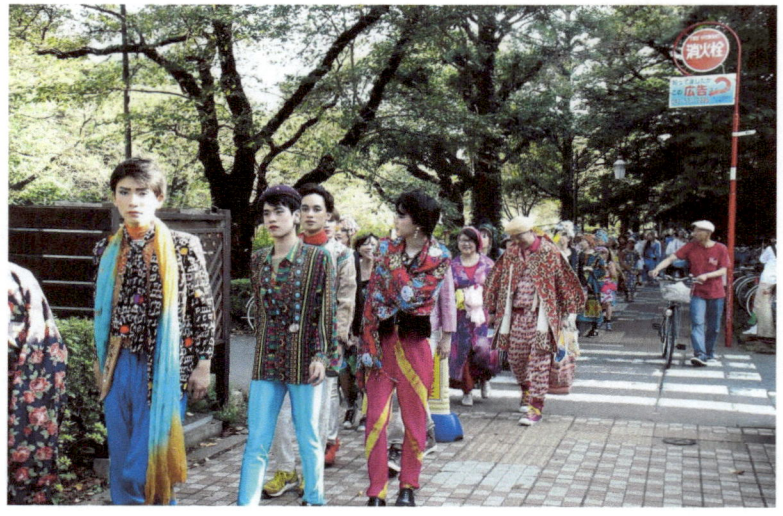

Another view of the Parade

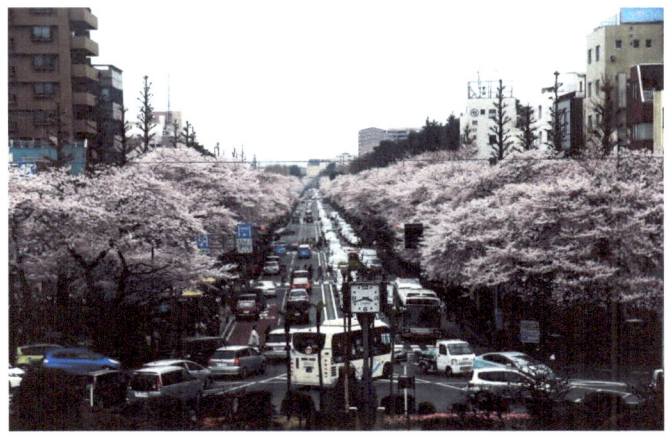

Ariel view of where the Kunitachi Parade,

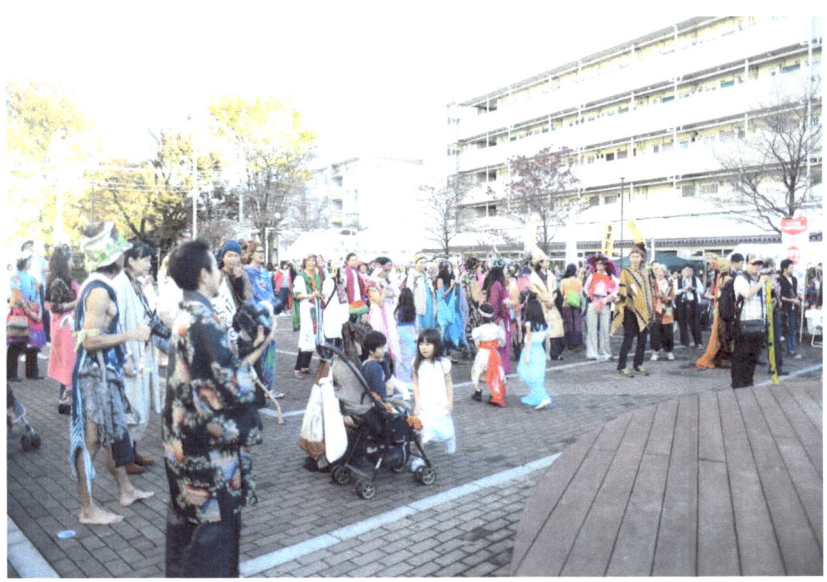

Audience waiting for the show of Majical Rainbow
adapted from Della Burford book Magical
Earth Secrets - to love and protect the earth.

Kunitachi Parade
to show our own unique selves!
We will be colorful at the parade!

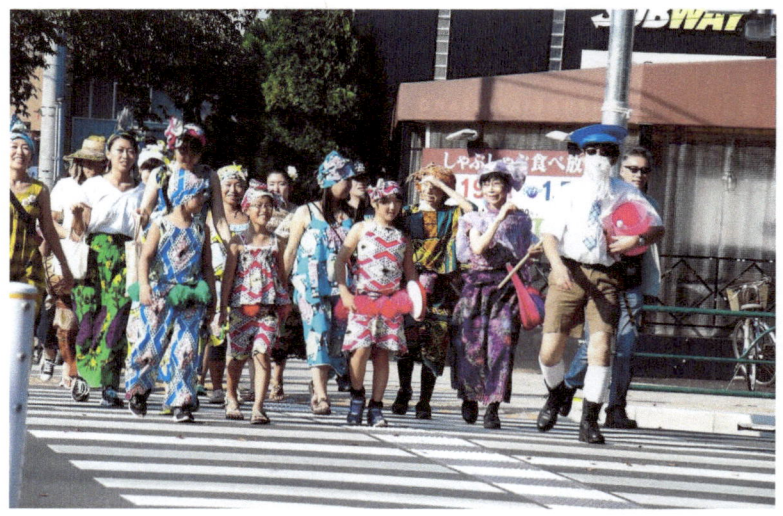

Colorful costumes in group Parading

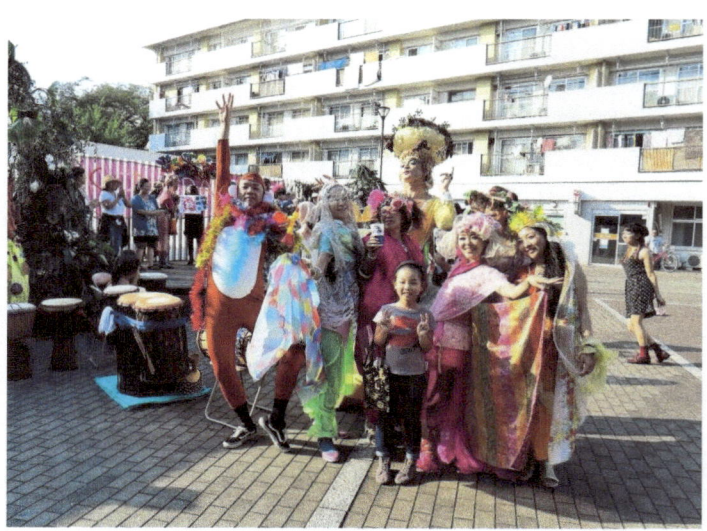

100% Parade 2016
We will play music at the Parade!

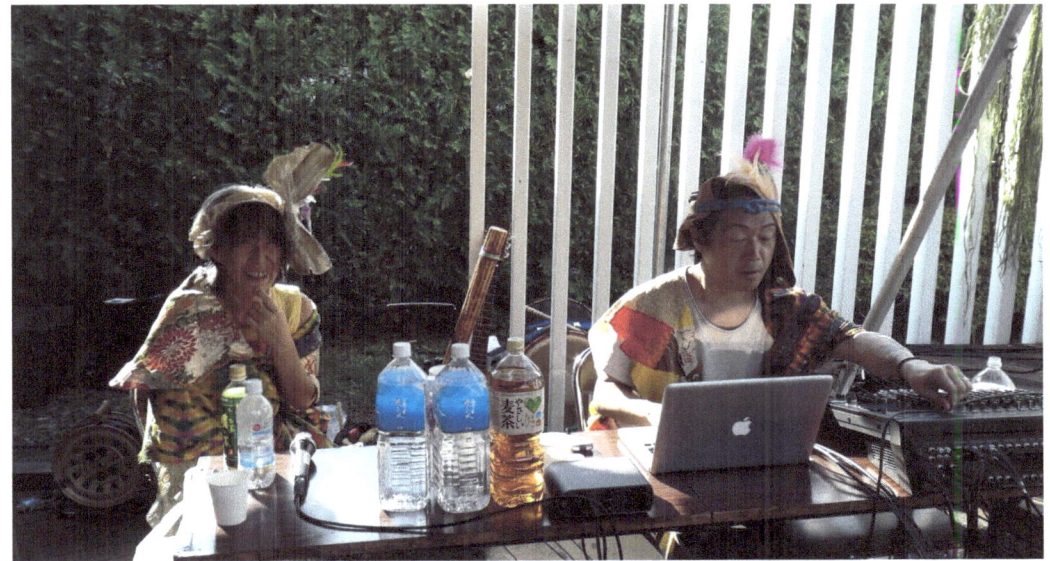

We will dance at the Parade!

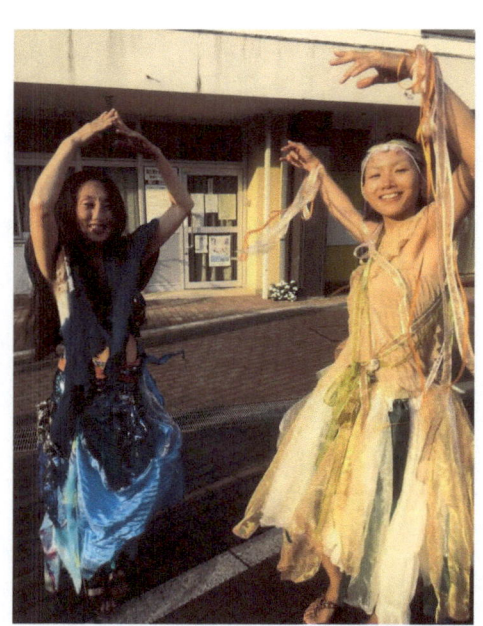 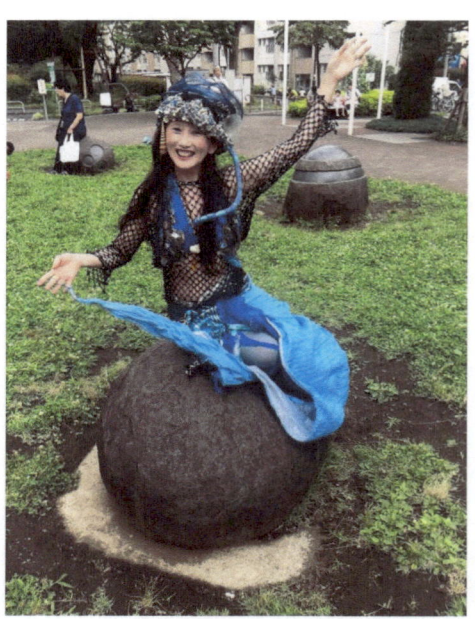

Majical Rainbow at the Kunitachi Parade 2016 from book "Magical Earth Secrets" by Della Burford

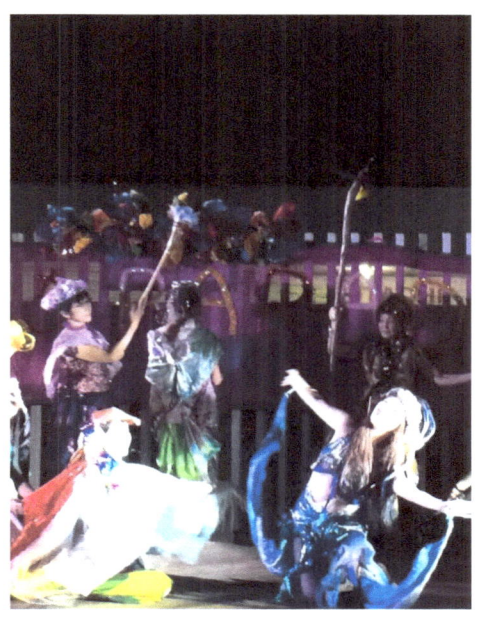

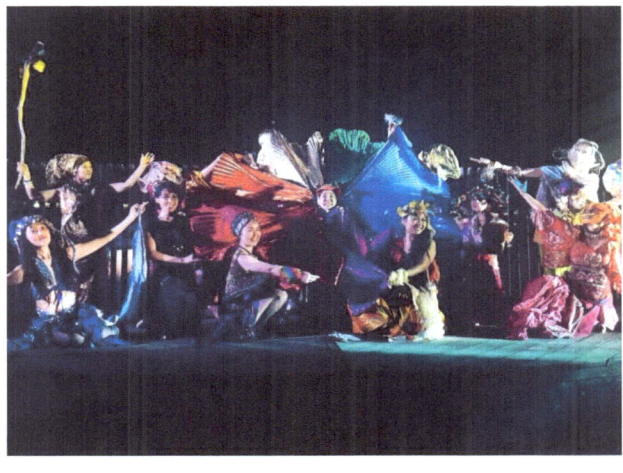

Eagle Child with full rainbow.

A Musician and Singer at the Kunitachi Parade

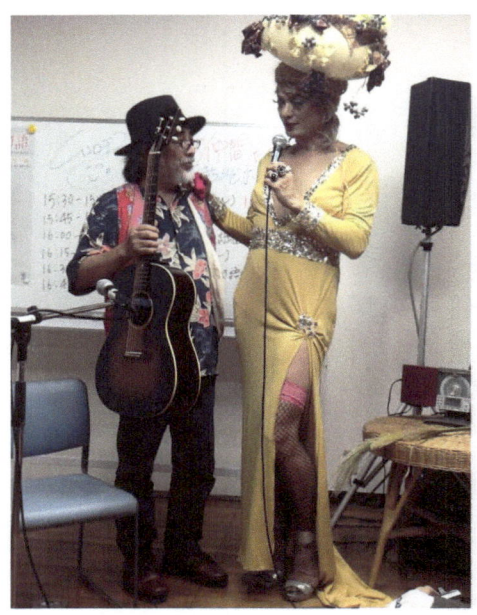

The Parade in On!

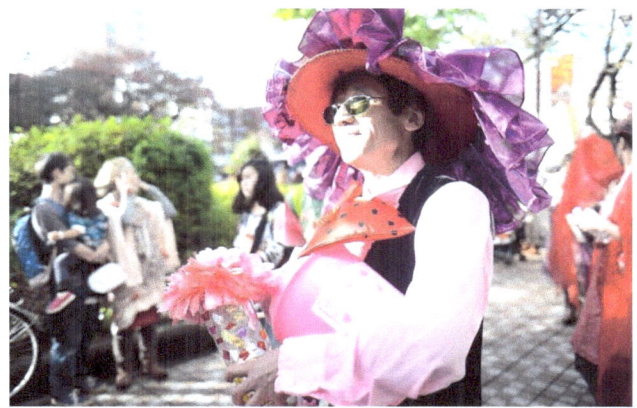

The parade is on!

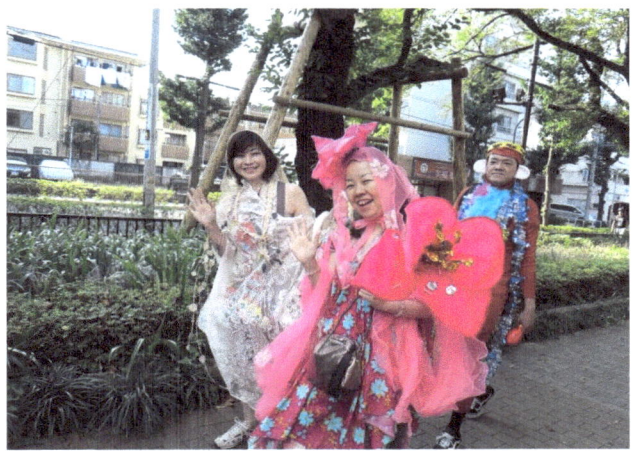

Coming to the parade!

2017 Lets make this a Joyful Parade!

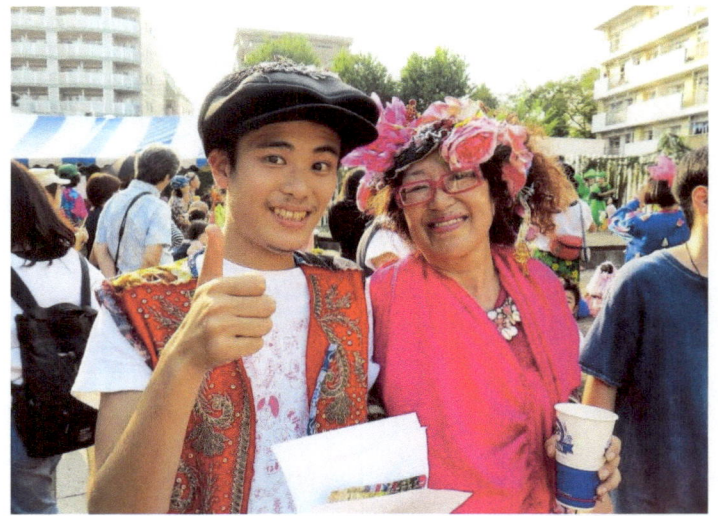

Mui Miyama Kona and Ruu*Ruu at the parade

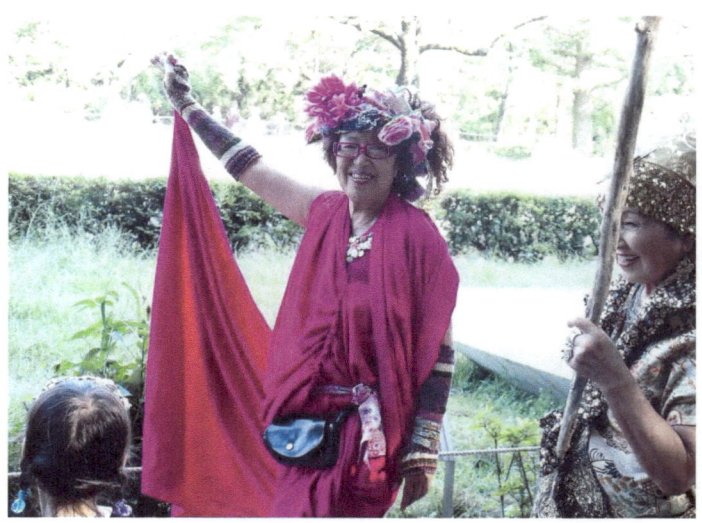

Ruu*Ruu and Kazuko - Kunitachi Parade

The Kunitachi Parade !

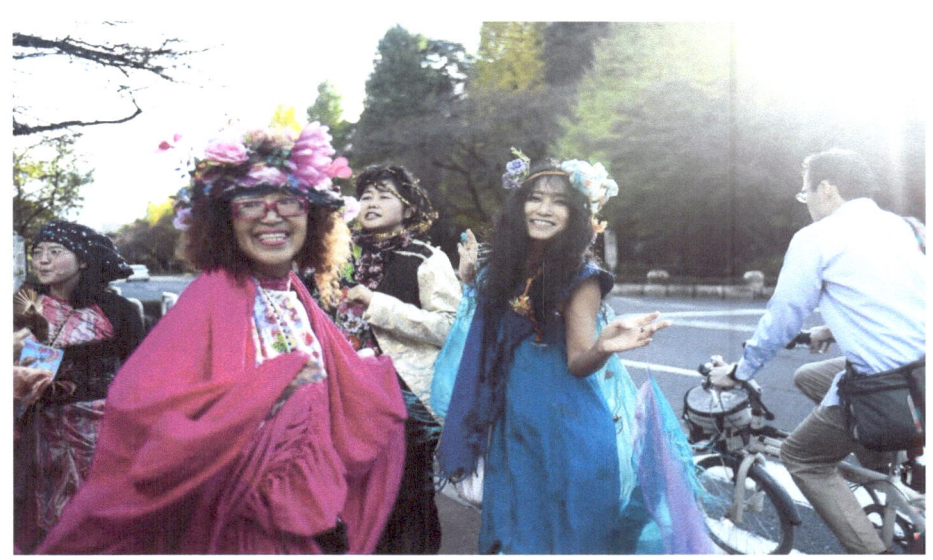

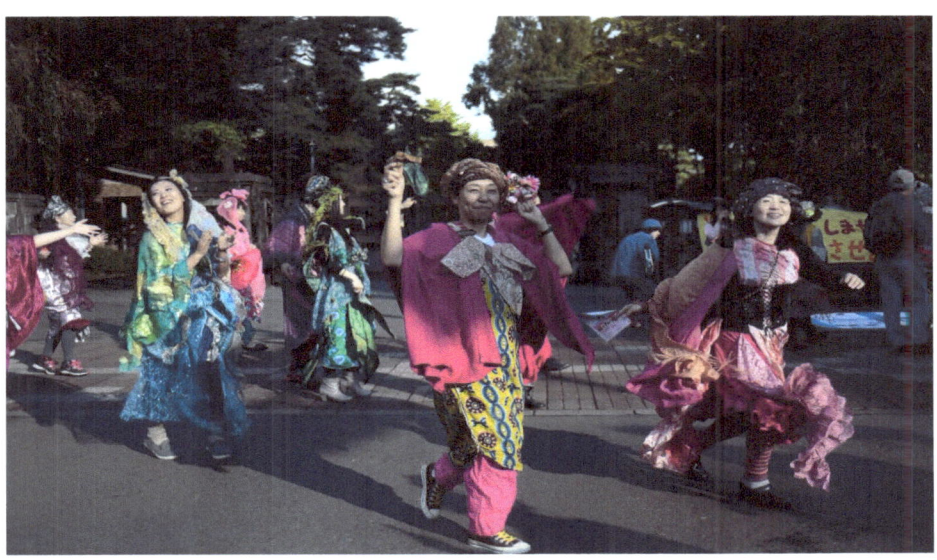

We can all Parade.. put a hat on, the right attitude and off you go!

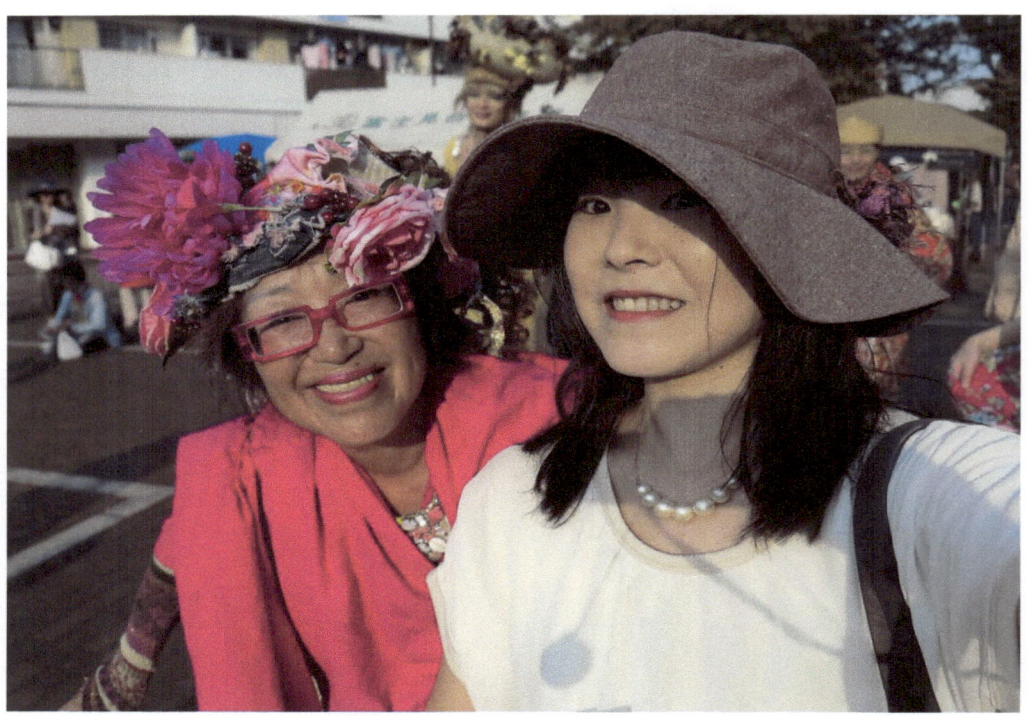

Preparing for the Parade

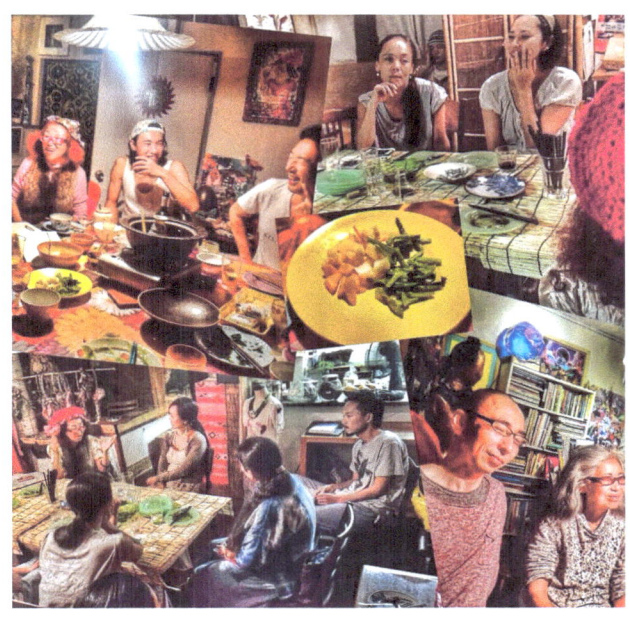

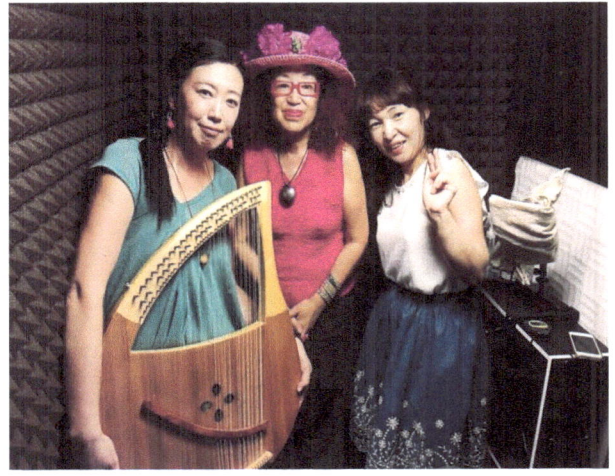

Poetry at the Parade
Poetry for Peace

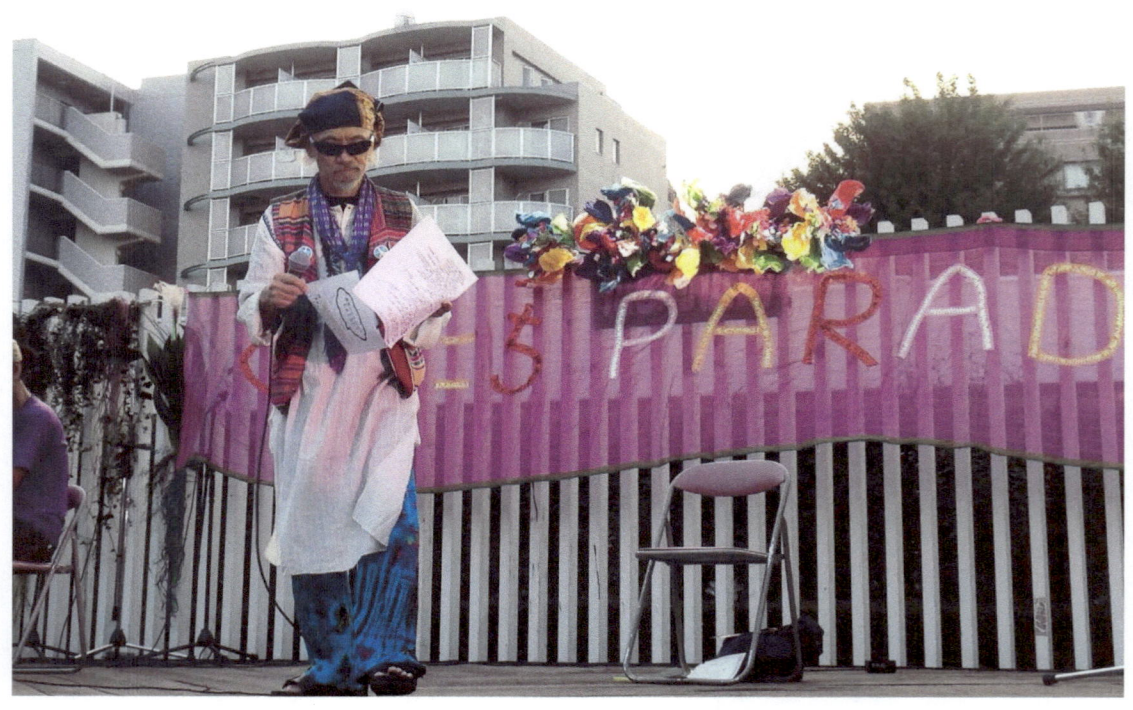

Poet photo by Unemisa

Women Poets at the Parade

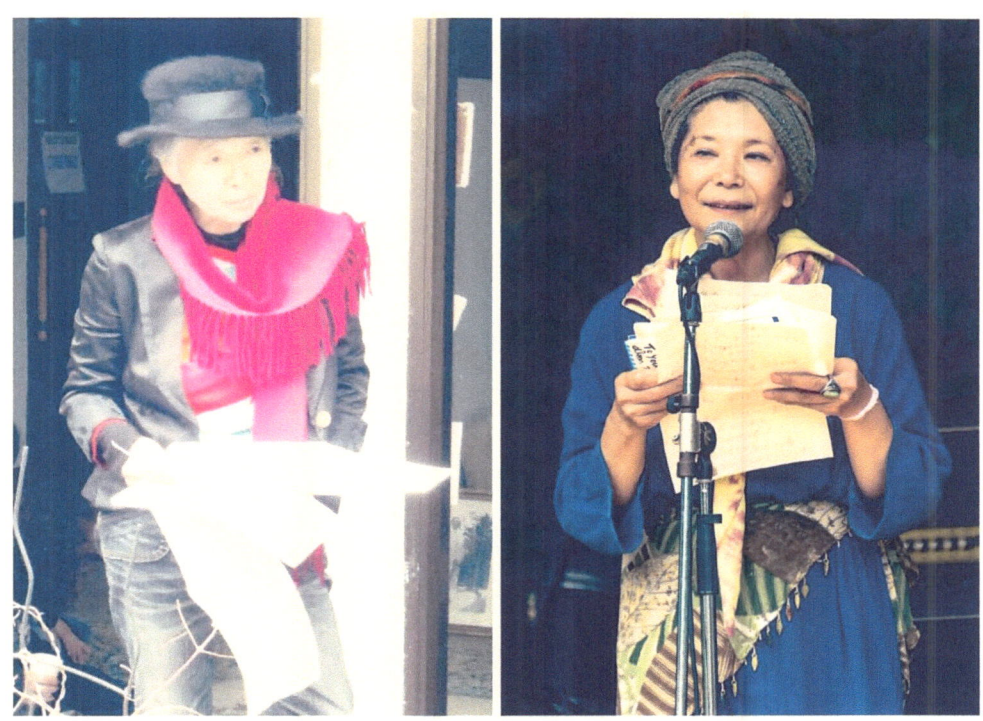

2017 Cooperative Show

Everybody came together to make this a special event!

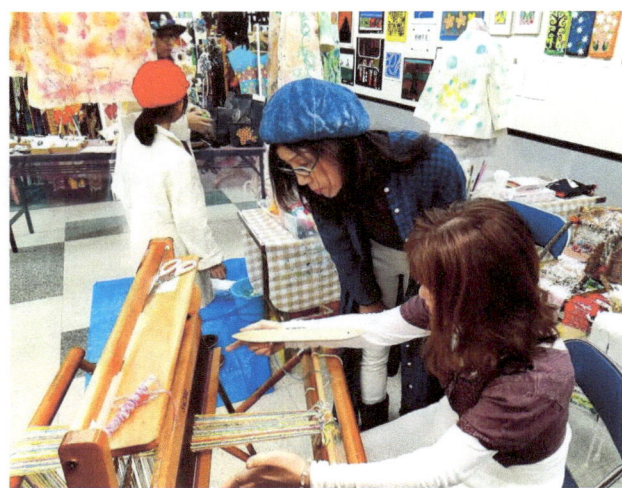
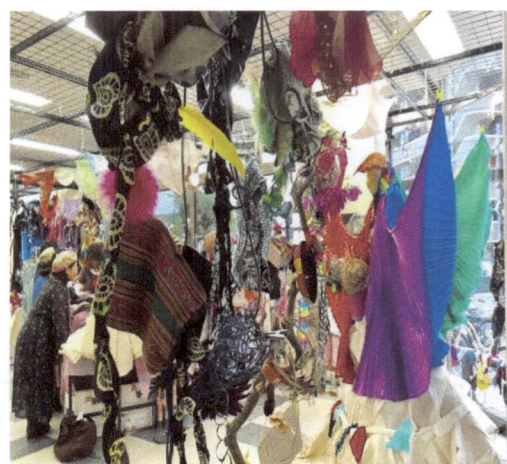
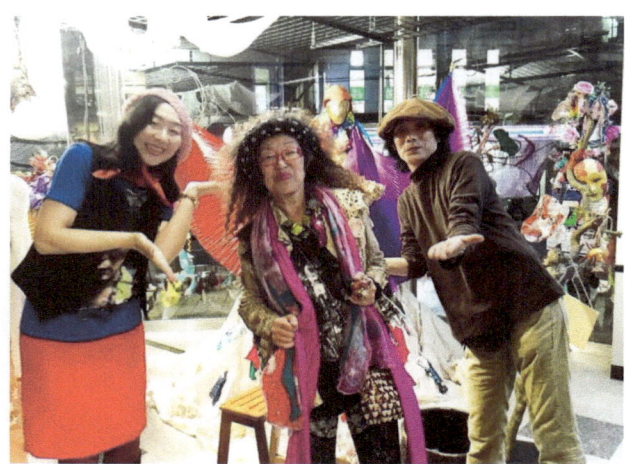
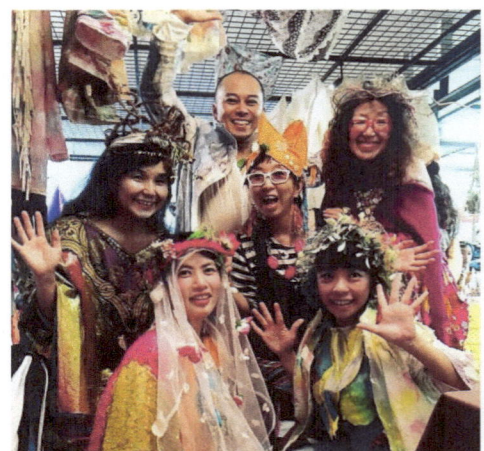

Majical Rainbow group together to love and protect our earth.

"I and the earth are one
I love the earth and will protect the earth"

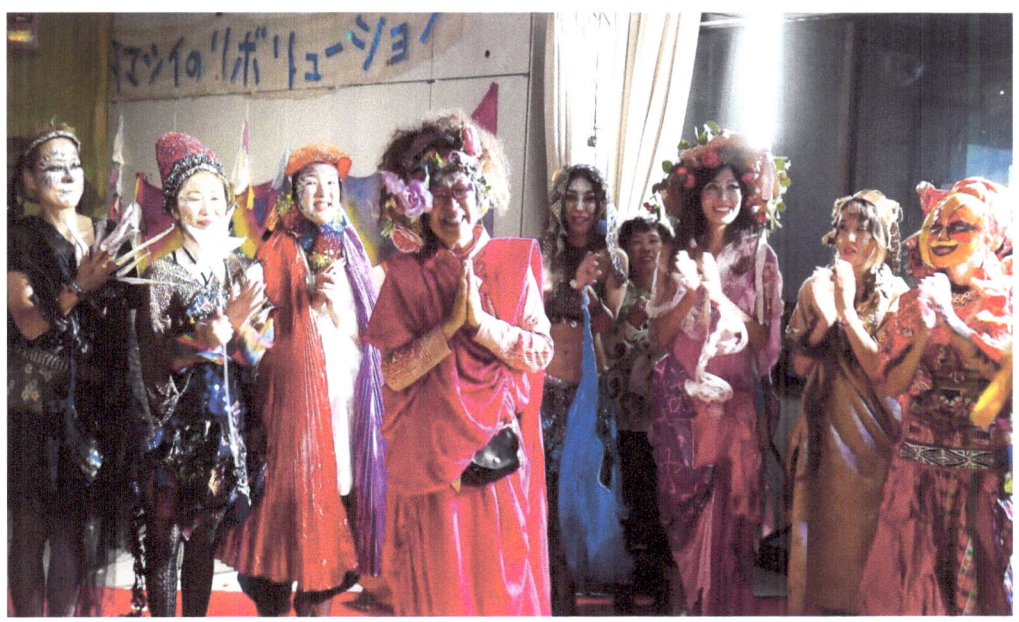

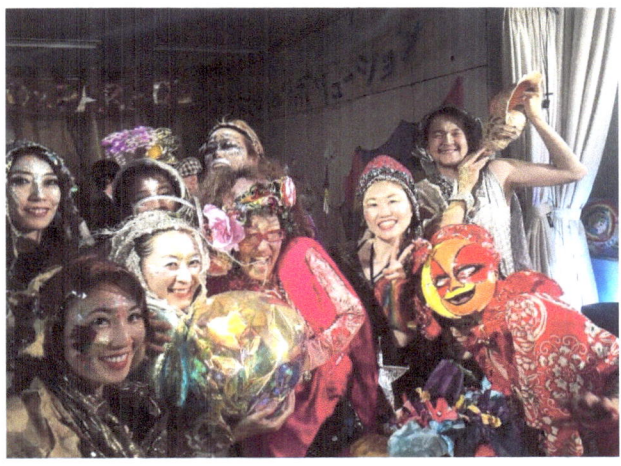

Thanks to all the performers of "Majical Rainbow"
from the book by Della Burford "Magical Earth Secrets"

Hiroko Ishizuka painting up a storm & giving workshop

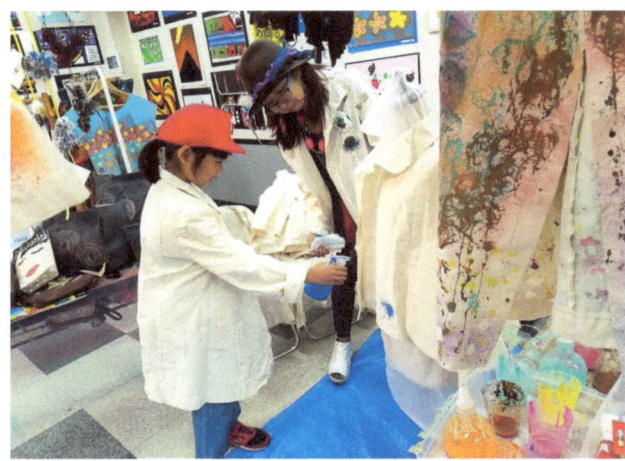

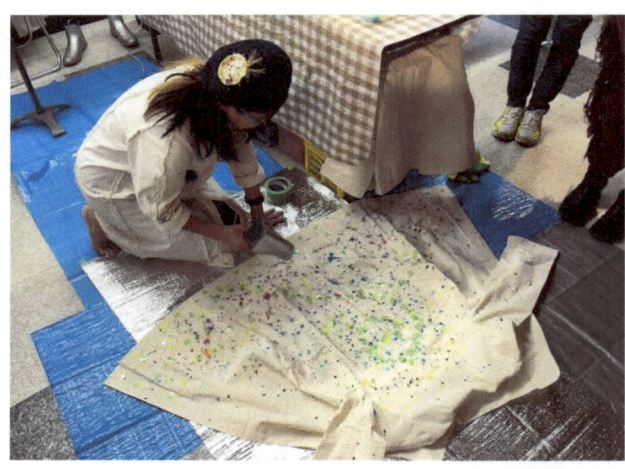

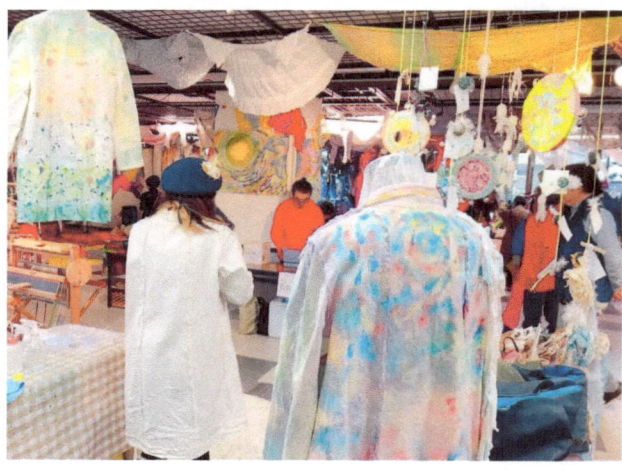

Meeting/Sharing at the "Inside Parade"

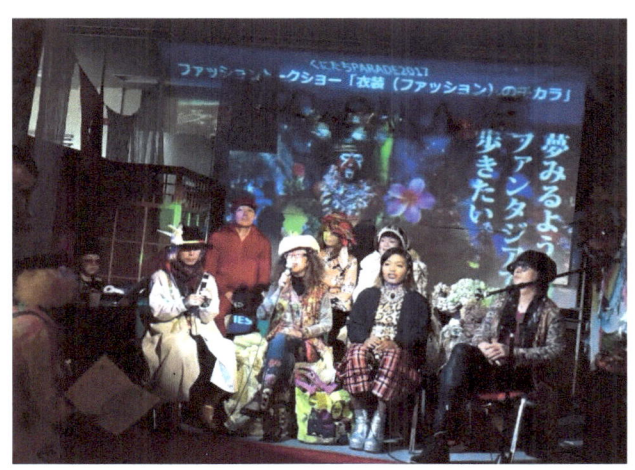
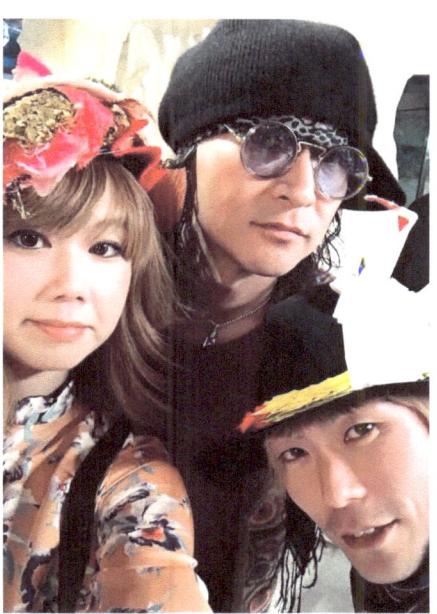
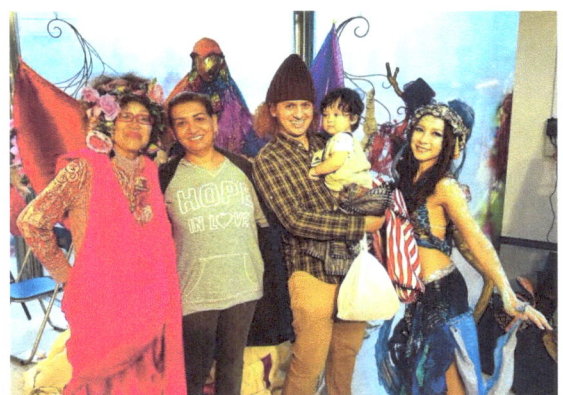
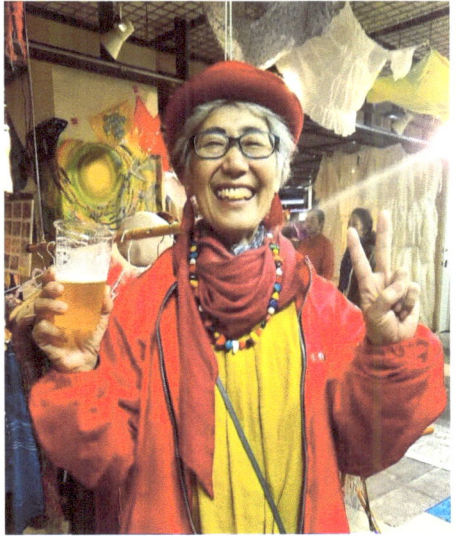

Many designs are being done for fun!

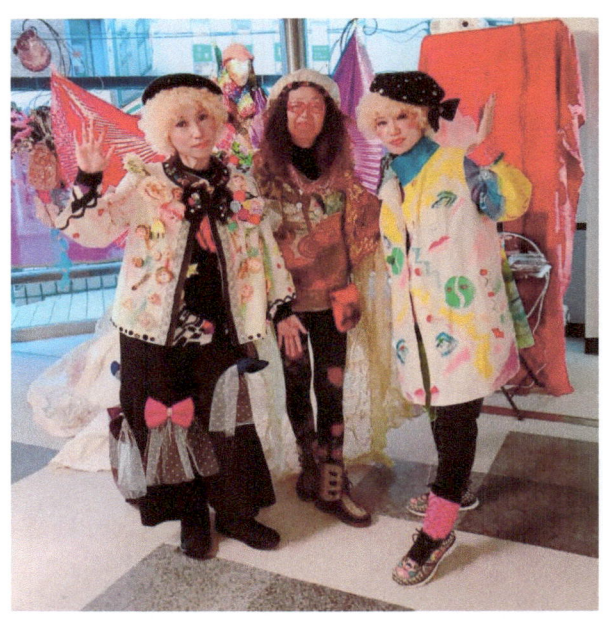

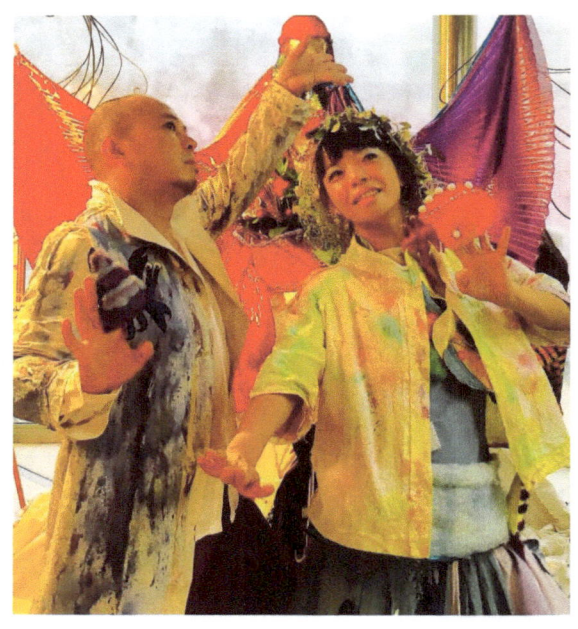

2017 - Ruu*Ruu & Musicans/Singer

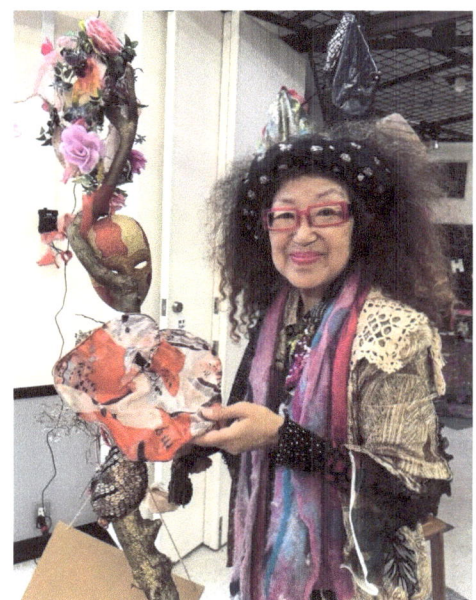

Ruu*Ruu

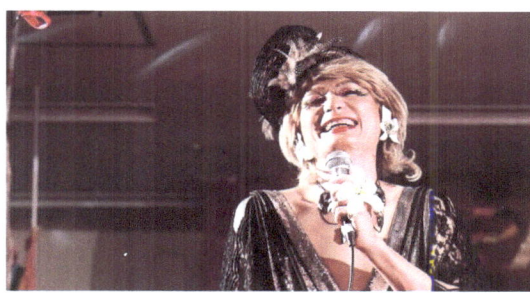

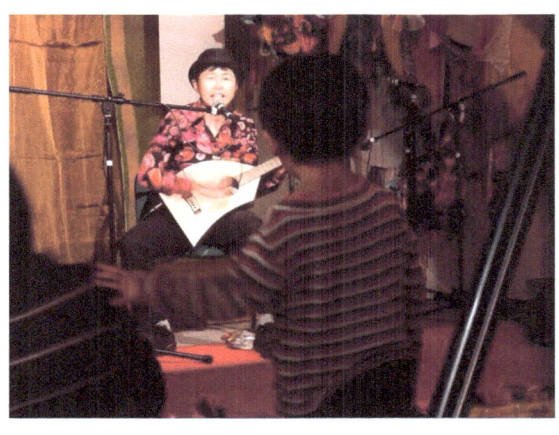

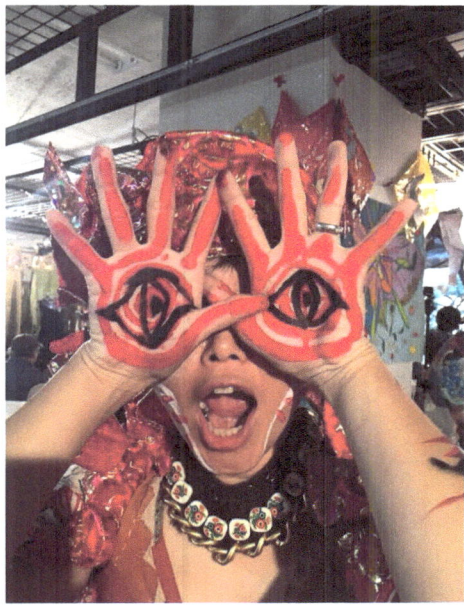

Dress up time.. lets have fun!

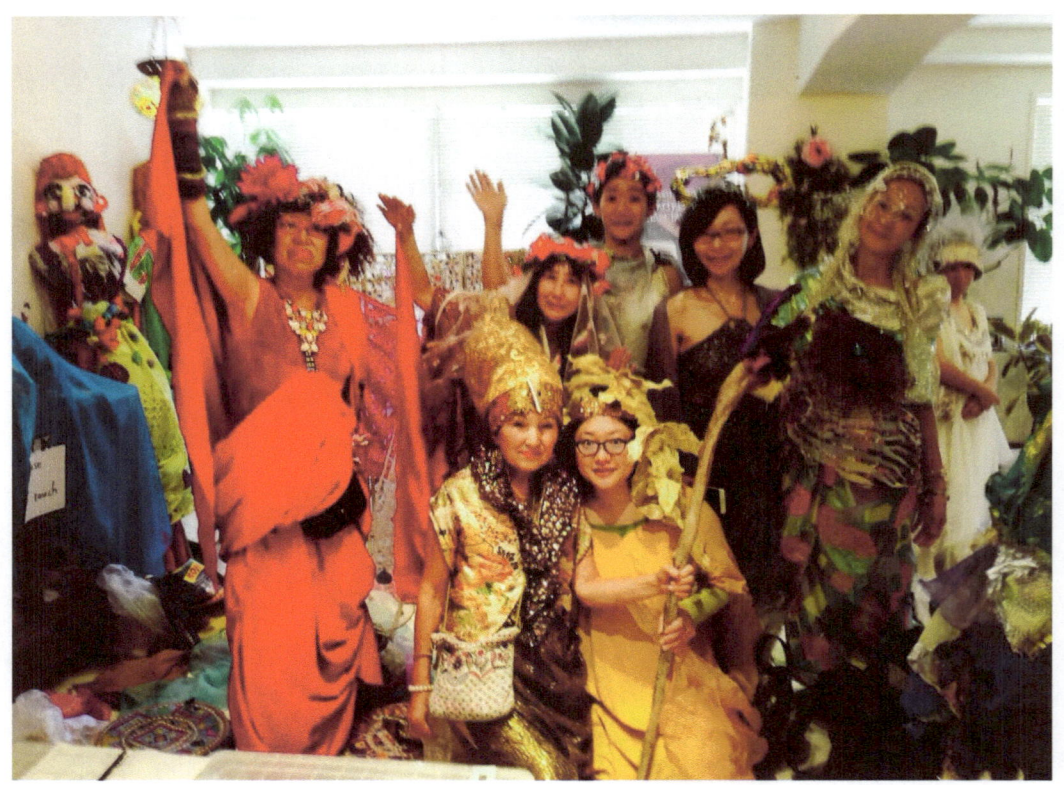

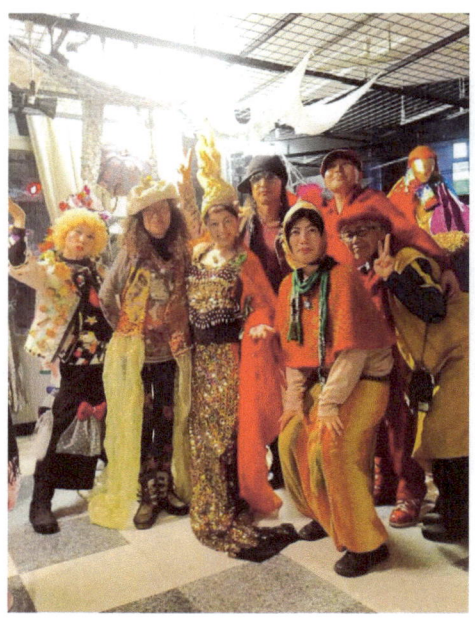

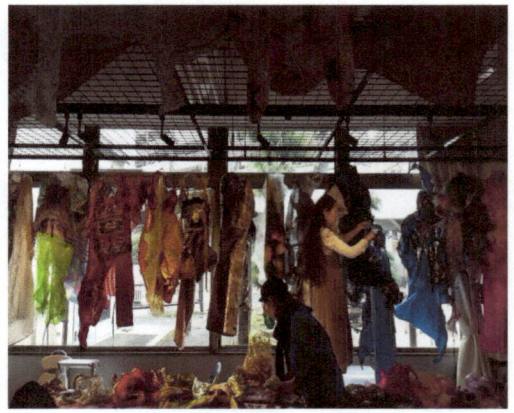

More artists at the Event!

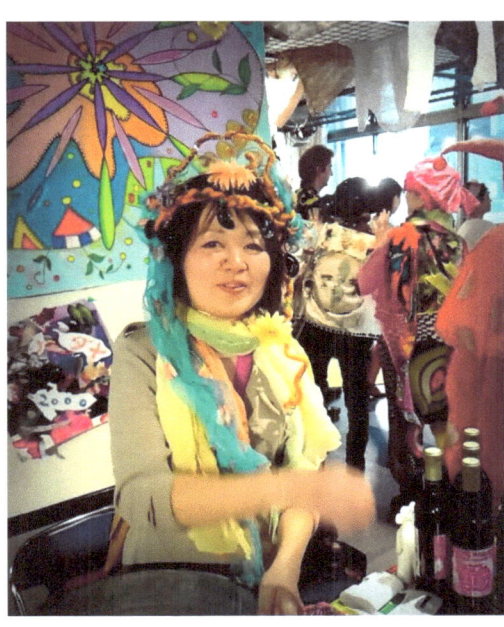 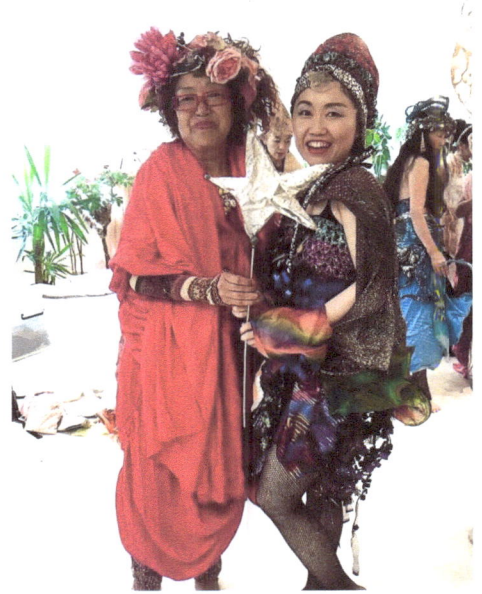

"honor your dreams by manifesting them"
2017 - Performance - Majical Rainbow

Lively 100% Parade group in costumes for the Majical Rainbow - adaption from the book Magical Earth Secrets. by Della Burford, Costumes by Ruu*Ruu.

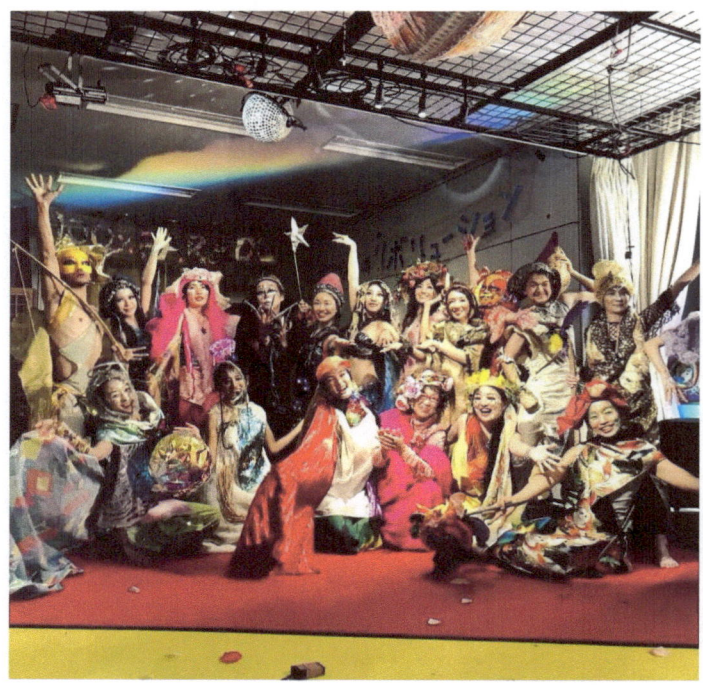

Kanazawabunko Art Festival

Each year since 2012 of Magical Rainbow has been performed. This is a huge art festival with booths and entertainment. For 20 year the Festival happens every year and is just about to happen with an opening performance of Majical Rainbow on September 16th 2018.

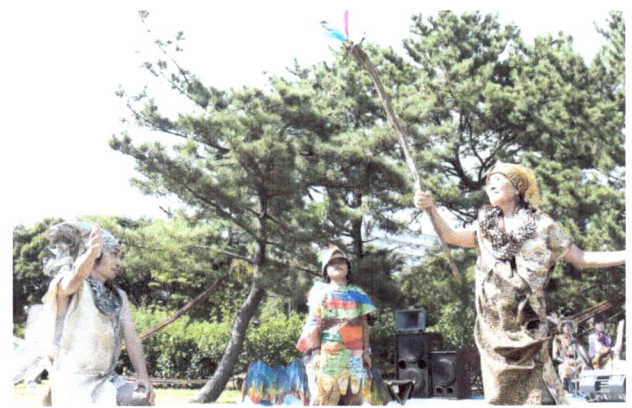

One of the first performances of Majical Rainbow at the Kanazawabunko Festival

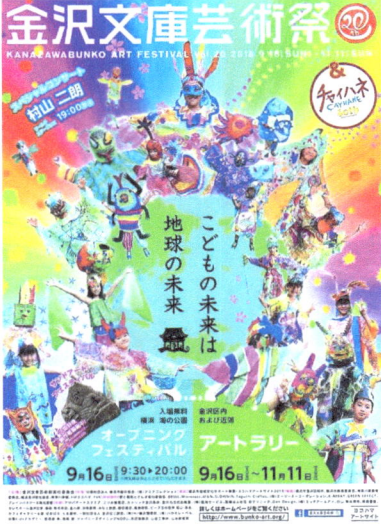

Poster for the Kanazawabunko Festival 2018

"This is a live dream"
Kanazawabunko Festival Poster

We could hardly believe the colors, life and good energy in this poster. When arriving and going to the Festival we saw the children & performers in their beautiful costumes and the same good energy, colors and life was bursting from eveywhere. We had arrived at a place of our dreams.

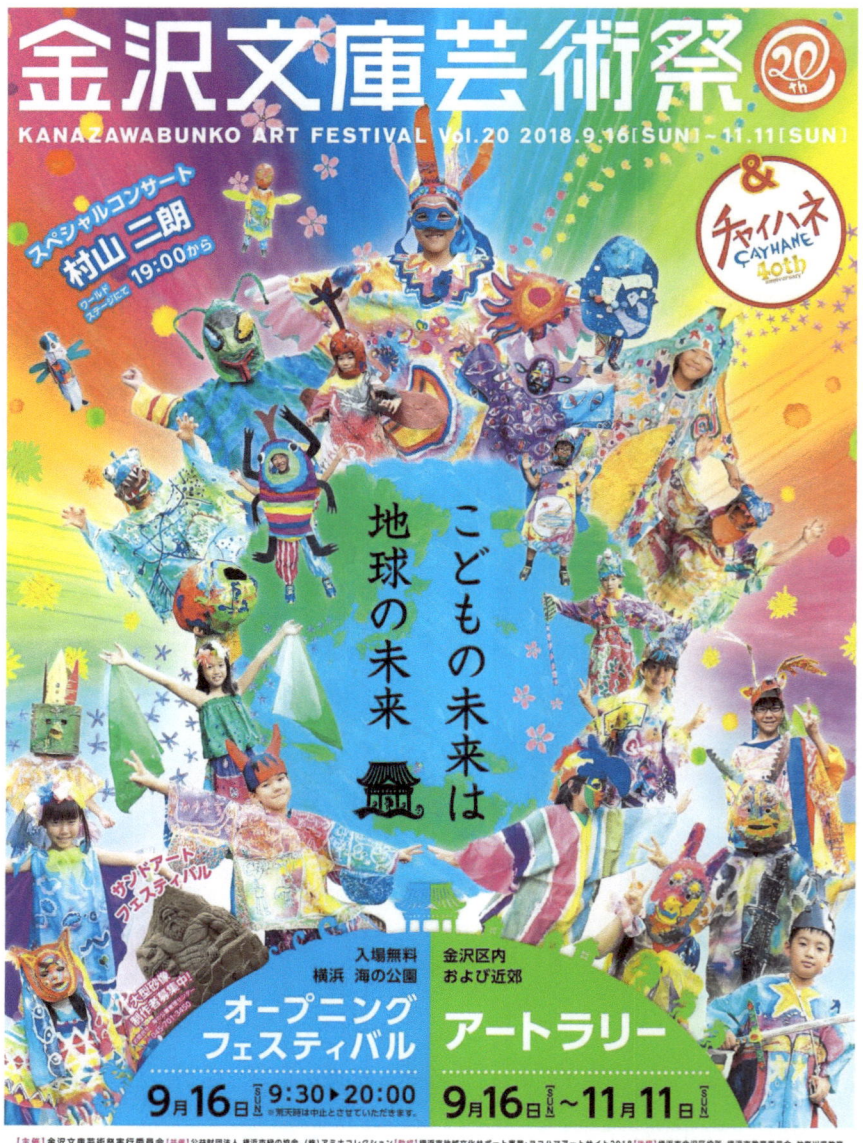

2018 Kanazawabunko Festival

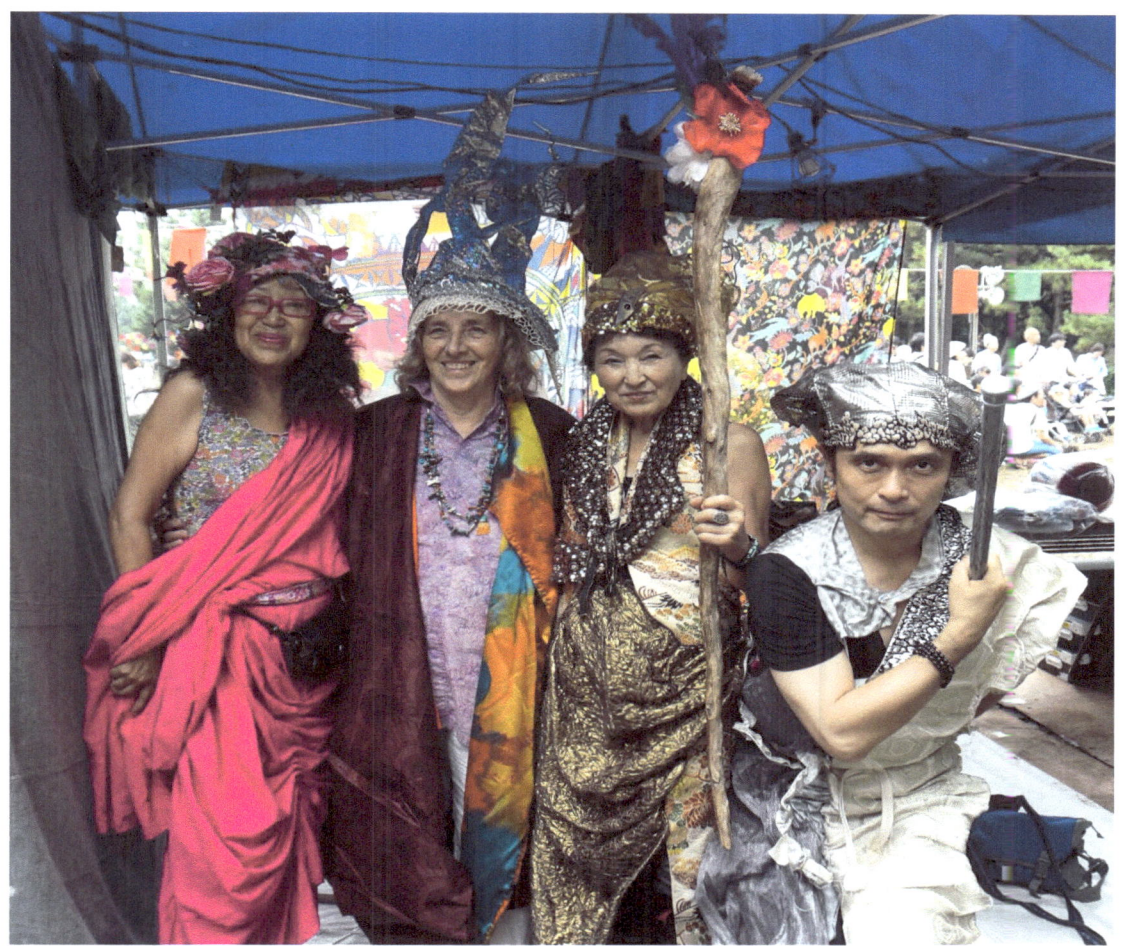

2018 - Della & Dale in Japan

Dale and Della visited Japan. They went to the Kanzawabunko Festival and saw 20 performers in Magical Earth Secrets called in Japan "Majical Rainbow". Ruu*Ruu's costumes were awesome and the performance magnificent.
It was truly magical.

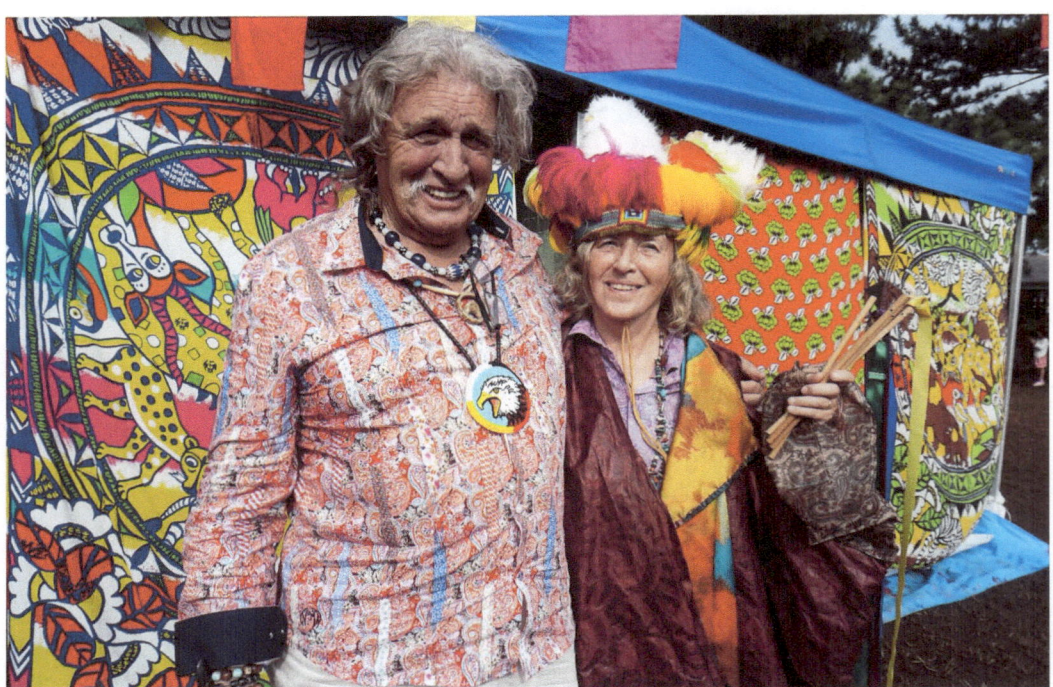

2018 - Majical Rainbow live!

"Majical Rainbow" makes the book "Magical Earth Secrets" become alive!

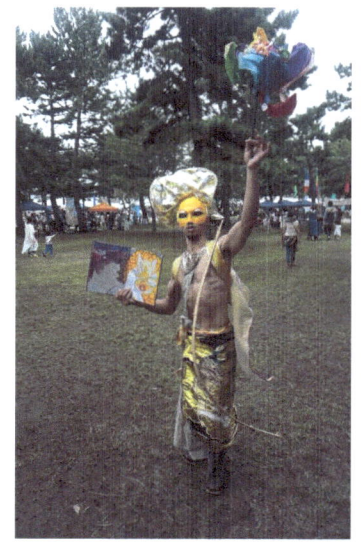

Satoru Ugajin as SunRay

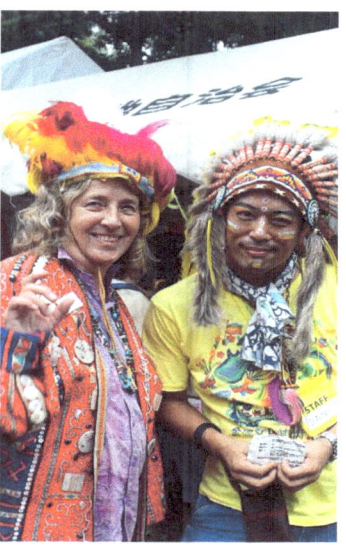

Della and Dan Asaba

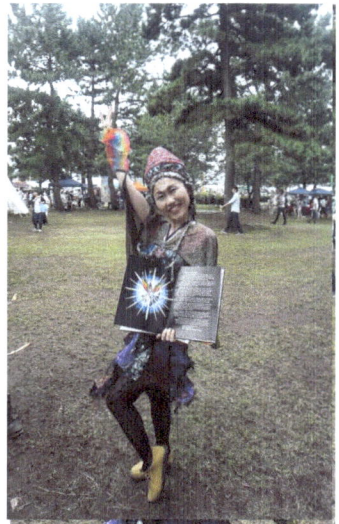

Tomomi Shimizu as StarBird

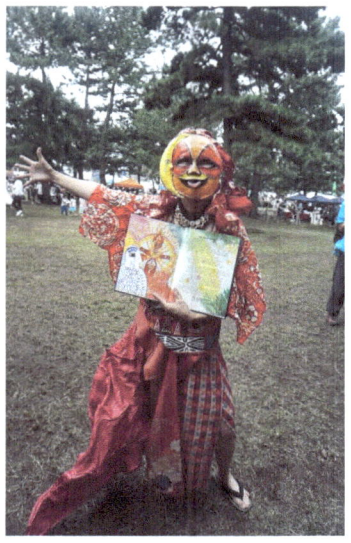

Ricky Risa Nishizawa as Earth Seed

2018 Performers are together!

All the performers are together to perform "Majical Rainbow". They look beautiful costumes designed by Ruu*Ruu. They are ready to give a message to love and protect the world.

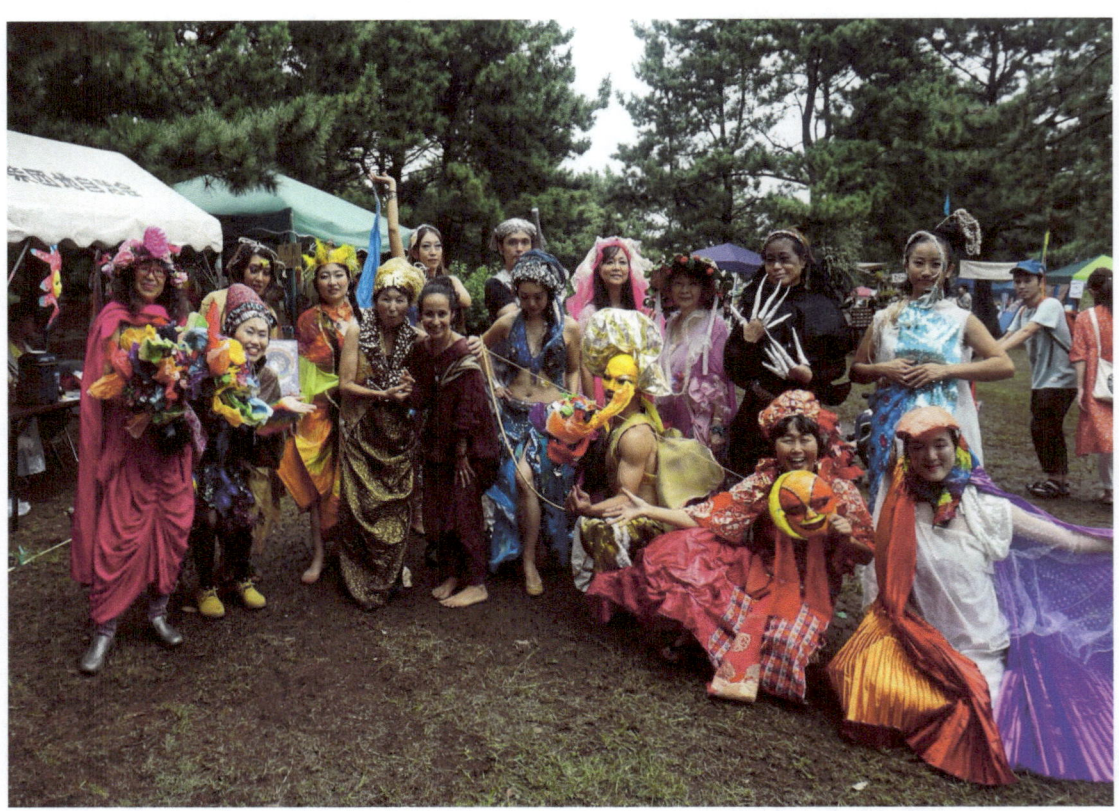

Ruu*Ruu, front Tomomi Shimiza, Kazuko Asaba with a friend, Yuhki Oomoto, Satoru Ugajin, Ricky Risa Nishzawa, Momoko Suda, and in the back from right to left Yuki Ishio, Masa, Yu Spring, Tazuko Noguchi, Susumu Tamura, Satri Abe, Uoomin Asami and Hiromi Inti Uezmi- missing is Yuko Nawa Inui and Fiori Hanawo the - musician. etc.

"Ruu*Ruu had a dream of making " God ornaments
Tokyo - Visiting Ruu*Ruu's Studio

Dale and Della visited Ruu*Ruu in Tokyo and saw her studio. We all saw some new designs for costumes Ruu Ruu is making for Della"Burford'd story "Miracle Galaxy" which is the story of the eight healing Angels. Many are Goddess - like and come from dreams. Our wish is that this book will inspire you to make creative costumes or Parade for Joy, Peace or Love.

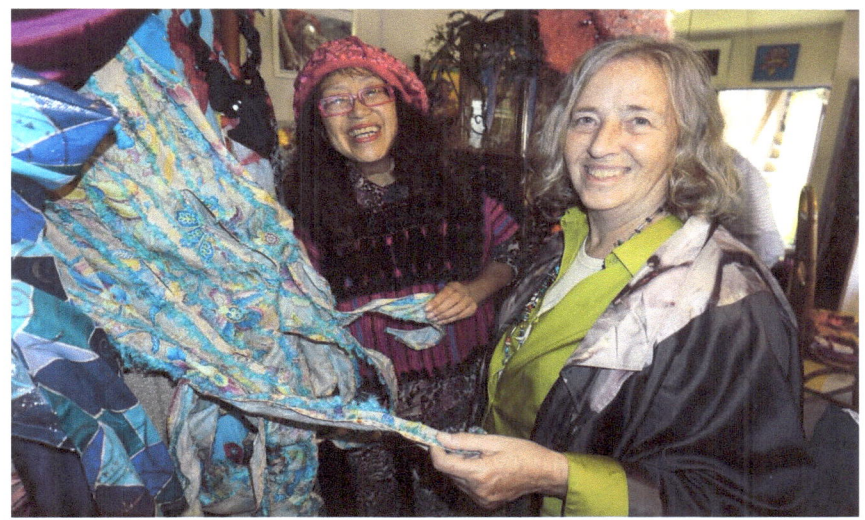

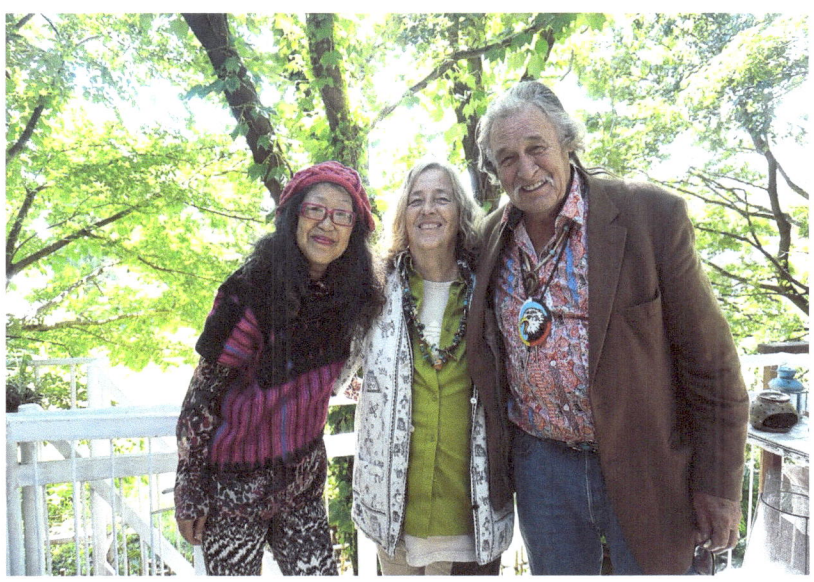

Tribute to Kazayuki Mitani

Tribute to Kazayuki Mitani who is now in the Spirt Worfd thanking him for the energy he put into the 100% Parade and performing the Sun Ray in Majical Rainbow.
Your Spirit will shine for us forever!

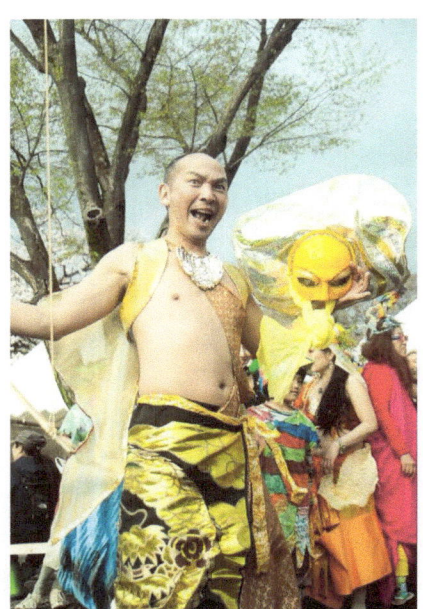 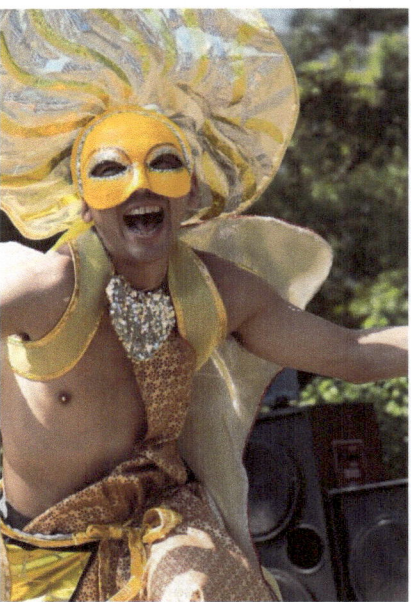

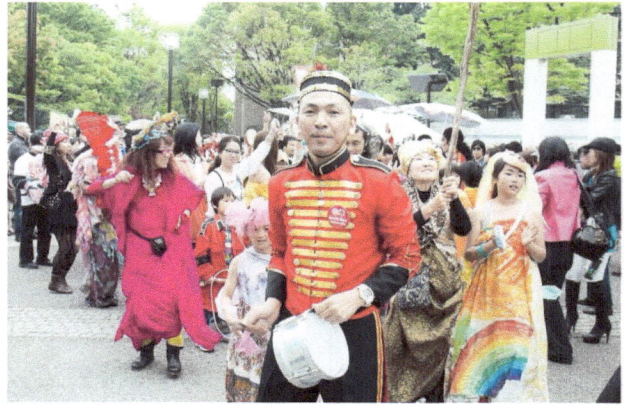

www.ingramcontent.com/pod-product-compliance
Lightning Source LLC
Chambersburg PA
CBHW051212220526
45473CB00003B/999